QUANTITATIVE DEVELOPMENT IN INFANCY AND EARLY CHILDHOOD

Quantitative Development in Infancy and Early Childhood

Kelly S. Mix
Janellen Huttenlocher
Susan Cohen Levine

OXFORD
UNIVERSITY PRESS

2002

OXFORD
UNIVERSITY PRESS

Oxford   New York
Auckland   Bangkok   Buenos Aires   Cape Town   Chennai
Dar es Salaam   Delhi   Hong Kong   Istanbul   Karachi   Kolkata
Kuala Lumpur   Madrid   Melbourne   Mexico City   Mumbai   Nairobi
São Paulo   Shanghai   Singapore   Taipei   Tokyo   Toronto

and an associated company in Berlin

Published by Oxford University Press, Inc.
198 Madison Avenue, New York, New York 10016

www.oup.com

Oxford is a registered trademark of Oxford University Press.

Library of Congress Cataloging-in-Publication Data
Mix, Kelly S.
Quantitative development in infancy and early childhood / Kelly S. Mix, Janellen
Huttenlocher, and Susan Cohen Levine.
p. cm.
Includes bibliographical references and index.
ISBN 0-19-512300-X
1. Number concept in children. I. Levine, Susan Cohen.
II. Huttenlocher, Janellen. III. Title
BF723.N8 M58   2001
155.42′234—dc21   00-039951

9 8 7 6 5 4 3 2 1

Printed in the United States of America
on acid-free paper

To our greatest teachers—our children

Acknowledgments

We are indebted to many people who made the publication of this book possible. First, we would like to thank our students and collaborators who helped to shape our thinking about quantitative development over the years. Special thanks to Nora Newcombe of Temple University and Arthur Baroody of the University of Illinois for invaluable comments on previous drafts of the entire manuscript. Thanks also to Linda Smith of Indiana University for contributing her expertise to Chapter 9. We are grateful to Rijenna Murray for her assistance with permissions and other administrative tasks. Finally, we thank our husbands, Brian, Peter, and Michael, for giving us the extra time and support we needed to make it happen.

K. M.
J. H.
S. L.

Contents

QUANTITATIVE DEVELOPMENT IN INFANCY AND EARLY CHILDHOOD

Historical Trends and Current Issues

In this book we present an overview of early development in the quantitative domain, a central aspect of human intelligence. Our goal is to bring coherence to the burgeoning literature on quantitative development from infancy through the early school years when children acquire basic mathematical conventions. This topic is important because mathematical skills are vital to successful functioning in our increasingly complex, technological society. Furthermore, quantitative development has been a focus in the ongoing theoretical debate concerning the origins of cognition and the availability of innate competencies.

This book reviews the evidence concerning the nonverbal quantitative skills of infants and young children. We identify key issues raised by the extant findings and hope to set an agenda for future research. Moreover, we find support for a new account that we believe captures development across the entire early childhood period better than the current alternatives. Before moving on to a topical presentation of this material, let's set the stage with a brief historical look at research in quantitative development.

A Brief Historical Review

For years many believed that quantitative reasoning emerged late in the preschool years. This belief seemed well-founded. Children generally do not demonstrate conventional number skills (e.g., counting, calculating with number facts, etc.) until preschool age or later. Because younger children and infants show few signs of quantitative reasoning in a conventional sense, it was easy to believe that the underlying abilities did not exist. Furthermore, Piaget (1941/1965) found that preschoolers fail a variety of nonconventional tasks that involve quantitative invariance. For example, in his number conservation task, children were shown two arrays with the same number of items. Then the items were spread out or moved together so that one array was longer than the other. The child's task was to recognize that the arrays remained numerically equivalent despite these changes in spatial arrangement. Not until school age are most children able to do so. Findings such as this led many to conclude that preschoolers lack the basic understandings essential to a mature concept of number.

Since then, much research has challenged this portrayal of the preschooler as numerically incompetent. First, researchers have found evidence of early quantitative competence even though these preschoolers have not yet mastered conventional number skills. For example, Gelman and Gallistel (1978) observed that even young children who do not know the conventional count words reveal an understanding of the principles that define counting. These authors noted that while many young children may at first count using idiosyncratic tags, such as "one, two, six . . ." or even "A, B, C . . .," there are still relatively few errors of one-to-one correspondence in tagging items to be counted, and the same sequence of tags adopted by a particular child is consistently used. Furthermore, they contended that children demonstrate understanding of the cardinality principle through emphasis or repetition of the final tag used in a count. Thus, children seem to understand the basic ideas behind counting even before they have learned the conventional count word sequence.

Researchers also have argued that Piaget's conservation task underestimated preschoolers' abilities. One criticism is that it has a strong verbal component. To answer correctly, children must interpret relational terms, such as "more," "less," and "same as." Subsequent research has shown that many young children do not know what these terms mean (Donaldson & Wales, 1970; Rothenburg, 1969). Indeed, when quantitative invariance tasks are presented without this linguistic requirement, preschool children demonstrate competence at an earlier age (Braine, 1959; Gelman, 1969, 1972).

A second criticism of Piaget's approach has been that when the spatial transformation is carried out in full view of the child, it is too salient to ignore. This may lead children to say the arrays have changed because they were so captivated by the transformation that they attribute undue importance to it. Similarly, they may assume that the transformation was relevant or else the adult experimenter would not have emphasized it. When procedures are used that deemphasize the salience of the transformation, young children are more likely to respond appropriately (e.g., Bruner, Olver, Greenfield, et al., 1966; Gelman, 1969, 1972; Mehler & Bever, 1967; Wallach, Wall, & Anderson, 1967). On the basis of these findings, it appears that preschoolers have greater quantitative competence than previously assumed.

The evidence of early ability provided by these preschool studies led researchers to ask whether they could tap numerical ability in even younger children using other experimental techniques. A common approach has been to test whether infants can discriminate between small set sizes using the habituation procedure. It has been found that, over a sequence of trials, infants become less attentive to a small set of a particular numerosity and then recover atttention when they are shown a set of a different numerosity (e.g., Starkey & Cooper, 1980; Strauss & Curtis, 1981). This pattern is true even of neonates (Antell & Keating, 1983). The infant literature also contains evidence of calculation ability (Simon, 1992; Wynn, Hespos, & Rochat, 1995). Specifically, researchers have found that when infants witness a quantitative transformation of a hidden array (e.g., seeing one doll added to a set behind a screen), they look longer at an incorrect than a correct solution.

These findings reveal quantitative awareness at an age far younger than that predicted in Piaget's framework. Understandably, this work has had a significant impact on theories of quantitative development. Some have posited an innate mechanism for representing and transforming number in infancy (e.g., Starkey, 1992). Some have even claimed that infants can quantify small sets of discrete entities exactly (e.g., Wynn, 1998). This view contrasts significantly with the previous idea that quantitative competence does not emerge until early childhood (Piaget, 1941/1965). However, as we will see, a close examination of the existing evidence does not support such a dramatic change.

Current Issues in the Study of Quantitative Competence

Recent findings have suggested new ways of thinking about quantitative development. However, rather than definitively explaining the origins of quantitative competence, these studies have raised unresolved questions. These questions, which we outline below, are the focus of this book.

First, how should we interpret the evidence of quantitative sensitivity in infants? Are infants sophisticated quantitative reasoners whose abilities were not tapped by previous measures? Or are infants' abilities limited precursors of childhood competence? In some accounts, one is left with the impression that infants possess the fundamental skills of mature numerical reasoning (e.g., Gallistel & Gelman, 1992; Starkey, 1992; Wynn, 1998). Subsequent development seems to consist of little more than the gradual expression of these skills in increasingly complex and explicit tasks. The idea of exact number evaluation in infancy is a radical shift from early theoretical views. Thus, we need to define precisely what quantitative competence actually has been demonstrated. Does the existing evidence lead to the conclusion that infants represent discrete number exactly? Likewise, we should define if and how infants' notions of number differ from those of young children. Contrary to the infant work, there is evidence of weaknesses as well as strengths in preschool children's number concepts. Most of the work on this question has focused on discrete quantity. We review and evaluate this research in the early portion of the book, chapters 2–4.

Much less investigation has focused on sensitivity to continuous quantity. Still, there are major questions concerning whether infants are sensitive to discrete quantity, continuous quantity, or both, and how these different notions relate to one another throughout early development. Natavists have argued that discrete number concepts are privileged, whereas continuous quantity concepts are not. However, several recent findings indicate that infants are sensitive to continuous amount (e.g., Gao, Levine, & Huttenlocher, 2000; Huntley-Fenner & Carey, 1995). In chapters 5 and 6, we review this literature and discuss the relation between early understandings of discrete and continuous quantity. We consider whether a common mechanism or different mechanisms are involved in quantitative tasks involving discrete number and continuous amounts. Such questions can be addressed only after the parameters of competence on tasks involving both types of quantity have been defined.

A consideration of early sensitivity to quantity raises the question of underlying processes. How is it possible for infants and young children (and indeed nonhuman animals) to perform quantitative tasks without the benefit of a conventional system? Several models have been proposed. These, like most research in early quantitative development, have focused on discrete number. Some are based on the use of a rapid perceptual process that is linked to spatial individuation (e.g., Trick & Pylyshyn, 1994) or the gestalt form of the sets to be enumerated (e.g., Mandler & Shebo, 1982; vonGlasersfeld, 1982). Others invoke the use of a nonverbal enumeration process analogous to verbal counting (e.g., Gallistel & Gelman, 1992; Meck & Church, 1983). More recently, accounts based on the use of object representations have been developed (Simon, 1997; Uller, Carey, Huntley-Fenner, & Klatt, 1999). All of the above processes are thought to emerge in infancy. A contrasting view posits that exact representation of number does not emerge until preschool age. However, this depends not on conventional counting but on nonconventional symbols (Huttenlocher, & Jordan, Levine, 1994). In chapter 7, we review the evidence for each proposed account and also discuss its compatibility with the overall picture of quantitative development that emerges from the literature reviews in chapters 2 through 6.

The final question considered in this book concerns the transition from nonverbal quantification to conventional skills. Specifically, how do mathematical conventions, such as counting, map onto preexisting quantitative representations? Once the facts of early competence with discrete and continuous quantities have been established, we can consider the relations and transitions between quantitative competence in children of different ages. A basic assumption of most work on quantitative development is that early abilities serve as a meaningful precursor of later skills. Some even claim that the quantitative processes available from infancy provide a sufficient framework for acquisition of conventional number systems (e.g., Gallistel & Gelman, 1992; Gelman, 1991). Others hold that early nonconventional mechanisms and conventional quantitative systems are structured differently. In this case, learning quantitative conventions is thought to be difficult and protracted due to interference from the preverbal mechanisms (Wynn, 1995). Yet a third possibility is that an understanding of verbal counting and other conventions is not built directly on early quantification but instead arises from repeated exposure to the conventions themselves. In chapter 8, we discuss these issues and the literature related to them.

The picture of quantitative development that emerges from our examination of the literature is quite different from that proposed in some current views. As we will see, although infants are sensitive to quantity, some of the stronger claims of early competence are not supported. In particular, the literature provides no clear evidence that infants represent discrete number exactly. Hence, there is no reason to conclude that number is a privileged domain or even to assume that the origins of quantitative reasoning are number based. There is, however, mounting evidence that infants can represent overall amount and that they use this sensitivity to perform quantitative tasks. Thus, an alternative starting point seems possible—that continuous and discrete quantities are initially undifferentiated. Such a representation would be adequate for most quantitative tasks, given that number and amount tend to covary. However, children would need to differentiate the two in order to understand conventional enumeration and mathematics. Thus, a major milestone in this view is the realization that discrete and continuous quantities are distinct. The preschool literature already provides evidence related to this achievement. Specifically, this differentiation may be linked to the emergence of conventional and preconventional symbolic processes in early childhood. In the chapters that follow, we present a review of the evidence that leads to this alternative account. We hope that this will contribute to an understanding of the developmental course by which children become mathematically competent.

2

Quantification in Infancy

The idea that infants possess numerical understanding is relatively new. In fact, not long ago psychologists believed number concepts emerged at school age, when children conserved quantity and mastered the verbal counting system. However, new techniques for studying infant cognition have changed this view. There is now clear evidence of quantitative notions before school age. Indeed, even very young infants are sensitive to information about quantity. But does that mean infants have sophisticated numerical concepts?

As a result of these new findings, many researchers have been tempted to attribute high-level numerical reasoning to infants. However, as we will argue later in this chapter, such radical theoretical shifts are not necessarily supported by the data. First, let's consider precisely which abilities the infant studies have demonstrated. We will focus our discussion on three quantitative skills: (1) discriminating between set sizes, (2) recognizing equivalence and ordinality relations, and (3) understanding the results of quantitative transformations. Because most infant number studies have focused on discrete quantity, we restrict ourselves to that topic here and save our review of continuous quantity for chapter 5. However, as we shall see, this may be a false dichotomy when it comes to early quantitative development. In fact, estimation of continuous amount may play a larger role in development than many have believed.

Discriminating between Set Sizes

One of the first questions infant number experiments addressed was whether infants could discriminate between different set sizes. Previous research on pattern perception had demonstrated that when infants were shown pairs of displays that differed in set size (e.g., 32 vs. 128), they showed a significant preference for the larger of the two sets (e.g., Fantz & Fagan, 1975). This suggested that infants were sensitive to the quantity of elements in sets that are highly discrepant. However, these studies did not provide a good test of the ability to distinguish between specific quantities because they left open the possibility that infants' discriminations were based on differences in overall area, brightness, or contour length of the arrays, rather than numerosity per se.

To determine whether infants perceived more fine-grained differences in number, subsequent studies tested infants' discrimination between very small sets. Most of this work has used habituation, which capitalizes on the fact that when infants lose interest in a stimulus, they tend to look at it less. In habituation studies, infants are shown a series of stimuli that share a common characteristic, such as set size (e.g., all arrays of two items). If infants detect the commonality, their looking times will decrease over trials. At test, a novel stimulus is shown, such as an array of a different set size (e.g., three items). If infants display a significant increase in looking time when the novel stimulus is shown, they are said to *dishabituate*. This pattern is taken as evidence that infants perceived the invariant characteristic presented in the habituation trials and detected the novelty of the test stimulus.

Starkey and Cooper (1980) used habituation to test whether infants could discriminate between small sets close in number. These authors argued that by using small sets, they could test whether 4-month-olds, like adults and children, rapidly enumerate sets with less than five items. (This process, referred to as *subitizing*, is discussed in chapter 7). Starkey and Cooper presented two conditions. The first involved discrimination between two items and three items. These set sizes were chosen because they were within the subitizing range for adults and children. The second condition involved discrimination between four items and six items. These set sizes were chosen because they were beyond the boundary of the subitizing range but preserved the same ratio as the small number condition. Thus, the large number condition was intended as a control for discrimination based on nonnumerical cues, such as overall area. Furthermore, the items used in the arrays were arranged to ensure that discrimination was not based on either the overall length of the array or on the density of the items in the array (see figure 2.1).

Starkey and Cooper (1980) found that infants dishabituated in the

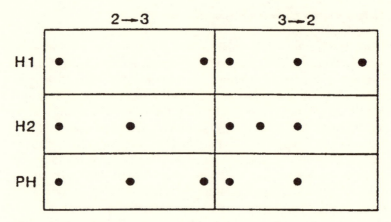

FIGURE 2.1 Representation of the stimuli used by Starkey and Cooper (1980). The labels H1 and H2 indicate habituation arrays and PH indicates the posthabituation arrays. Reprinted with permission from Starkey, P., and Cooper, R. G., Jr. (1980). Perception of numbers by human infants. *Science*, 210, 1033–1035. Copyright 1980 American Association for the Advancement of Science.

small number condition but not in the large number condition. That is, infants looked less and less at arrays with two items over trials and then looked longer when an array of three items was presented (and vice versa); however, this pattern was not obtained for comparisons of four versus six items. Starkey and Cooper concluded that infants cannot perceive the "absolute number" of more than three items. They further proposed that to discriminate between small sets, infants use the same subitizing process observed in young children because the range of numerosities discriminated by infants was within the subitizing range of young children.

In a subsequent study, Antell and Keating (1983) extended the work reported by Starkey and Cooper (1980). Their aim was to determine whether the numerical discrimination ability described by Starkey and Cooper was present from birth. To test this, they presented the same conditions to a group of infants ranging in age from 21 to 144 hours. Antell and Keating found precisely the same pattern of results as reported by Starkey and Cooper; neonates discriminated between small sets of discrete stimuli (2 vs. 3), but not larger sets (4 vs. 6).

Similar effects were obtained by investigators who varied the items in their displays in terms of size, type, and arrangement. Strauss and Curtis (1981) presented 10- to 12-month-olds with sets of color drawings (e.g., chicks, dogs, houses) arranged randomly on an imaginary four by four matrix. These drawings were photographed from one of six different distances to vary the size across displays. Half of the infants were habituated to slides that varied in item type, size, and position across trials (e.g., two large dogs, two small houses, etc.), and half were habituated to slides that varied in size and position across trials, but not item type (e.g., two small chicks, two large chicks, etc.). At test, infants were shown arrays of a novel numerosity, which consisted of either unfamiliar items for infants in the heterogeneous condition, or chicks for infants in the homogeneous condition. Three pairs of set sizes were compared: two versus three, three versus four, and four versus five. Strauss and Curtis found that, as in previous work, the infants in both conditions discriminated only two versus three items. Infants in neither condition discriminated between sets of four versus five. Results for the three versus four condition were ambiguous—certain groups of infants could discriminate between the sets under certain conditions. That is, female infants in the homogeneous condition and male infants in the heterogeneous condition successfully discriminated three from four items.

Similar results are reported for sets that were heterogeneous both within and across trials (Starkey, Spelke, & Gelman, 1990). In this study, the habituation displays consisted of aerial photographs of either two or three different household objects. At test, infants were shown a series of novel photographs that alternated between two and three items. During the test phase, infants looked significantly longer toward the numerically novel displays than they did toward the numerically familiar displays.

The sets in the studies described so far have all been static displays of photographs or drawings, but there is also evidence that infants discriminate sets of items in motion. VanLoosbroek and Smitsman (1990) habituated infants to small sets of rectangular figures moving continuously on a computer screen. At test, infants saw two trials of the familiar numerosity and two trials of a novel numerosity (i.e., the familiar numerosity either plus or minus 1). The same group of infants was tested at three age periods: 5 months, 8 months, and 13 months. At 8 months and 13 months, infants dishabituated to the novel number of moving rectangles. There was weak evidence of this ability at 5 months of age.

Taken together, the results of the habituation studies provide compelling evidence that infants can discriminate between visual sets presented all together. However, these discriminations may not be based on discrete number as is commonly thought. In most cases, when the number of items changes, the amount of stuff changes, too. For example, when one apple is added to two apples, the number of apples increases to three and, assuming the apples are roughly the same size, the amount of apple stuff increases by 50%. Unless differences in individual item size are extreme, attending to amount will lead to the same responses in discrimination tasks as attending to number. Thus, infants could discriminate two items from three items based on the contrast in overall contour length or surface area rather than the number of items.

To test whether this was the case, Clearfield and Mix (1999) habituated infants to arrays containing either two or three squares of the same size. At test, two alternating test arrays were presented: one with the familiar number of squares but a different amount of contour (i.e., the amount of edge accumulated over objects—see figure 2.2) and one with a different number of squares but the same amount of contour. Importantly, when contour length changed, the test amount was equal to what the contour length would have been if an object had been added or subtracted. This is analogous to the contour length change in previous habituation studies.

The results were clear. Infants dishabituated to changes in contour length when number of objects was held constant, but they did not dishabituate to changes in number when contour length was held constant. Because contour length covaries with area, brightness, and other perceptual variables, infants may base their discriminations on one or more of these other variables. Indeed, follow-up experiments using this procedure have revealed that infants dishabituate to changes in area, contour length, or both (Clearfield & Mix, 2000). The important point is that infants responded to amount of substance rather than discrete number in what seemed to be a number habituation task.

One might wonder, then, why infants failed to discriminate four versus six dots in Starkey and Cooper's (1980) large number control. Because four versus six is proportionally equivalent to two versus three, someone comparing the overall amount of stuff should be able to discriminate in both conditions. One possibility is that the process for estimating amount becomes too difficult to apply as sets increase in complexity. For example, if infants estimate quantity by scanning the contour of individual objects in a set, comparisons like four versus six would be more difficult than two versus three because there are more individual contours. This explanation is consistent with the finding that infants lose their ability to discriminate between displays as the complexity of the displays increases (e.g., McCall & Kagan, 1967).

The studies described so far have used sets of pictures presented simultaneously. However, infants' ability to discriminate between temporally distributed sets also has been tested. Wynn (1996) habituated infants to sequences that contained the same number of puppet jumps, either two or three. Infants viewed a series of these sequences, each separated from the next by the puppet's wiggling from side to side, until looking decreased to a set criterion. The rate and duration of sequences were varied so infants could not use these cues to discriminate between sets. At test, infants saw an alternating series of sequences with two and

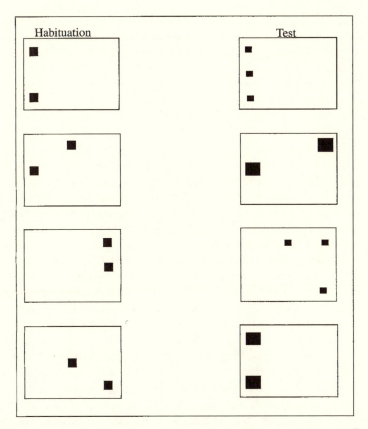

FIGURE 2.2 Sample stimuli from Clearfield and Mix's number habituation experiment. The test trials contrast number against contour length as the basis for discriminations. Reprinted with permission from Clearfield, M. W. and Mix, K. S. (1999) Number verses contour length in infant's discrimination of small visual sets. *Psychological Science*. Copyright 2000 Blackwell Publishers.

three puppet jumps. Wynn found that infants looked significantly longer toward the sequence that was numerically different from the habituation sequences.

Infants also have discriminated between temporal sequences in a visual expectation experiment. Canfield and Smith (1996) tested whether 5-month-olds could use the number of items appearing sequentially in one location to predict the appearance of additional items in a different location. Infants saw one of two repeating sequences of pictures on a computer screen. In one sequence, a certain number of pictures always appeared on one side of the screen before a picture appeared on the other side. For example, after two pictures were shown on the left side of the screen, a picture always appeared on the right side. Thus, it was possible to use the number of left side pictures to predict the appearance of the right side picture. In the other condition, infants saw the same pictures in an irregular sequence. In this case, infants could not use number to predict the appearance of pictures on the right side of the screen. The length of time each picture was shown was varied so infants could not use overall duration of the left side sequence as a predictor in either condition. Canfield and Smith found that infants who had seen the predictable sequence were more likely to shift fixation toward the right after the second left side picture than they were after the first left side picture. In contrast, infants who had seen the irregular sequence were equally likely to shift attention toward the right after either the first or second left side picture. These results suggest that infants can use quantitative information to predict the location of events in temporally distributed sequences.

The results of this experiment and Wynn's (1996) habituation task take on new theoretical significance, given evidence that infants use contour length or area to quantify object sets. Because these cues could not be used to discriminate sequences of events, studies using event sets may provide the only evidence that infants represent discrete quantity. However, further research is needed to confirm that this is the case. Aside from simply replicating the findings of these studies, additional study should rule out the use of nonnumerical cues. For example, previous research has established that infants are sensitive to changes in rhythm from an early age (Demany, McKenzie, & Vurpillot, 1977; Gibson, 1969). Because the rhythms in these number studies were not systematically varied, infants may have responded to differences in rhythm rather than in number.

In sum, infants' ability to discriminate between set sizes has been well established across a variety of experimental conditions. Several experiments have shown that infants from birth to 12 months of age react to changes in the set size of small static visual sets (Antell & Keating, 1983; Starkey & Cooper, 1980; Starkey et al. 1990; Strauss & Curtis, 1981). The same is true for sets of items in constant motion (vanLoosbroek & Smitsman, 1990). Furthermore, there is evidence that infants can discriminate between sets of temporally distributed events (Canfield & Smith, 1996; Wynn, 1996), even when the rate and duration of the sequences are varied. The remaining question is what forms the basis of these discriminations. Some have argued that infants use a counting-like process to represent and compare discrete quantities (Gallistel & Gelman, 1992; Wynn, 1995). However, the finding that infants use overall amount to discriminate object sets challenges this conclusion. As we will see, infants' use of amount may underlie performance on other quantitative tasks as well.

Recognizing Relations between Sets

In this section, we turn to studies that go beyond simple discriminations to test whether infants understand quantitative relations. One of the most basic quantitative relations is numerical equivalence. Understanding numerical equivalence means knowing that two sets are in the same numerical class even if they differ in every other way. For example, adults recognize that a set of two apples is equivalent to a set of two honks because both sets contain two items. This understanding has been tested in 7-month-olds using a cross-modal matching task (Starkey et al., 1990). Infants were shown pairs of visual displays that included one display of two objects and one display of three objects. While the displays were still visible, either two or three drumbeats were played. Infants responded by looking longer toward the display that matched the number of sounds. Starkey et al. concluded that infants can perceive the number of distinct entities both in a sequence of sounds and in a static visual display and can relate these sets to one another in terms of numerical equivalence.

Starkey et al.'s (1990) study received considerable attention because of its important claims and supporting data. However, the results of subsequent experiments have raised questions that challenge these claims. When Moore, Benenson, Reznick, Peterson, and Kagan (1987) attempted to replicate the cross-modal matching results, infants in their study showed a significant preference in the *opposite* direction. That is, infants looked longer at the display that was *not* equivalent to the number of sounds. Starkey et al. attributed this reversal to differences in statistical analysis (e.g., Moore et al.'s excluding infants who failed to inspect both displays), and differences in experimental procedure (e.g., Moore et al.'s allowing irritable or fatigued infants to take breaks between trial blocks). However, in a second replication attempt, infants again looked longer at the nonmatching display even when they were not given breaks and all infants were included in the analyses (Mix, Levine & Huttenlocher, 1997).

The reported effects were quite small in all three of these cross-modal studies. Because there were small effects in both directions, the reported effects may be spurious. That is, if an experiment is run enough times, the results should barely reach significance a few times by chance. Thus, the published studies might be in the tails of a normal distribution with many nonsignificant findings in the center. These nonsignificant findings would not necessarily be known because of the bias to publish significant results.

However, even if these effects represent a real preference, Mix et al. (1997) found evidence in a second experiment that this preference may not be based on number. Instead, infants could have matched to the overall rate and duration of the drumbeat sequences. Starkey et al. (1990) claimed that this was not possible because when they presented all of the drumbeat sequences at the same rate, infants showed the same small preference for the matching display, as did infants in a separate experiment where all of the drumbeat sequences were the same duration. However, this was not an adequate control because infants could have used duration information in one experiment and rate information in the other. In Mix et al.'s second experiment, rate and duration were randomly intermixed within the trials presented to each infant to ensure that rate and duration were not informative. Under these conditions, there was no preference for either the matching or nonmatching display; infants performed randomly when rate and duration cues were removed.

Whether the reported effects in these studies are attributable to chance or to the use of rate and duration, there reason to doubt that 7-month-olds can recognize numerical equivalence across sets presented in different modalities. However, is it possible that infants recognize numerical equivalence within the same modality? One might argue that infants' discrimination of numerosity in visual habituation studies provides evidence that they can. That is, in order to habituate to one set size, infants might be establishing an equivalence relation across the sets. Dishabituation to a novel numerosity could occur because infants recognize that the new set is not equivalent to the previous one. Although this may be possible, the results of the habituation studies alone do not provide sufficient evidence that infants are comparing sets. As Antell and Keating (1983) point out, "the ability to abstract invariant stimulus features and the discrimination of novelty based on such abstraction does not imply an understanding of the features by the infant or an ability to integrate information in a meaningful way" (p. 699). In other words, infants may simply recognize that a change has occurred, without necessarily knowing the nature of the change.

Next we turn to another quantitative relation—ordinality. Ordinal relations are central to the organization of number systems. For example, three derives its meaning not only from the number of entities it represents, but also from its relation to other numbers. Three can be described as the number that is one greater than two or seven less than ten. Recognizing these relations between numerosities is a crucial aspect of mature numerical understanding. However, only a few studies have evaluated infants' understanding of these important concepts.

Curtis and Strauss (1982, 1983, reported in Strauss & Curtis, 1984) tested whether 16- to 18-month-olds recognized ordinal relations in a discrimination learning experiment. Infants were shown pairs of displays that contained different numbers of red dots that varied in size and position across displays (e.g., one dot versus two dots). Over trials, infants were conditioned to touch the side of a display that contained either greater or fewer dots than the opposite side. Once an infant reached a criterion of either five consecutive correct responses or 30 trials, two transfer tasks were introduced. In one task, the previously reinforced numerosity was pitted against a novel numerosity. In the second task, two novel numerosities were pitted against each other. Infants were able to recognize ordinal relations, but only when they had been trained on the smaller number comparisons (one vs. two or two vs. three) and response to the smaller numerosity was rewarded (i.e., those infants trained to respond to "less than" relations).

Using a different approach, Cooper (1984) examined infants' recognition of ordinal relations with a habituation procedure. In this task, infants were habituated to pairs of displays presented in succession. In the "less than" condition, the first array in the pair was always less than the second array (e.g., infants saw a display of two items followed by a display of three items). In the "greater than" condition, the first array was always greater than the second array (e.g., infants saw a display of three items followed by a display of two items). At test, infants were shown four different pairings: (1) a previously seen pair from the habituation phase, (2) a novel pair that embodied the same relation as the pairs in the habituation phase, (3) a novel pair whose relation was opposite of the relation shown in the habituation trials, and (4) a novel pair in which the displays were equal in number. Cooper reported that 14- to 16-month-olds in the less than and greater than conditions "seemed to detect and remember these relations" (p. 163), presumably by showing dishabituation in response to test trials in which the opposite relation was presented. In contrast, 10- to 12-month-olds in these two conditions increased their looking times only for trials in which the pairs were equal, as if they had encoded the relation "different than" during the habituation phase, instead of "less than" or "greater than."

Further support for this interpretation comes from a second study reported by Cooper (1984) in which the same design was used but infants were habituated to pairs equal in number. At test, 10- to 12-month-olds looked significantly longer toward both greater than and less than test trials than they did toward equal test trials. This indicates that although infants did not detect specific ordinal relations, they could discriminate equality from inequality. Interestingly, 6- to 7-month-olds included in this experiment were slow to habituate and failed to show any consistent pattern of dishabituation, suggesting that even though performance in visual habituation studies might imply an understanding of equivalence relations, direct evidence of this ability does not appear until 10 months of age.

In summary, infants as young as 14 months old might be sensitive to ordinal relations, but there is a clear need for further study. Additional research is required to confirm the results reported by these authors, as well as to delineate the apparent constraints in terms of set sizes, direction of ordinality, and age level. Furthermore, in both the equivalence and ordinality research published to date, the displays have not been varied so as to separate the number of items from the overall amount of stuff. Thus, as in the habituation paradigm, responses that seem to be based on number might actually be based on estimates of amount.

Calculation: Understanding the Results of Numerical Transformations

At the heart of a mature concept of number is an understanding of the operations that transform number. Piaget (1941/1965) viewed the ability to distinguish numerically relevant from irrelevant transformations as a hallmark of quantitative development. Clearly, comprehending the results of numerical transformations is a vital prerequisite to learning conventional calculation algorithms.

Until recently, it was assumed that such understandings did not emerge until relatively late in childhood. However, more recent research has claimed that even young infants can anticipate the results of numerical transformations. Wynn (1992) showed 5-month-olds a small array that was then hidden. Next, she showed an item being added to or taken away from the hidden array. Infants could see the transformation take place, but they could not see the resulting array. For example, on the problem 1 + 1 = 2, infants were shown one doll and then a screen was raised to hide the doll (see figure 2.3). Next, a hand entered the display and deposited a second doll behind the screen. When the screen was lowered, either one doll (impossible outcome) or two dolls (possible outcome) were revealed. Wynn found that infants looked longer toward an incorrect solution than they did toward a correct solution.

Wynn's (1992) findings were replicated and extended in a study by Simon, Hespos, and Rochat (1995). These authors identified an important confound in Wynn's design, namely, that every arithmetically incorrect outcome also happened to be physically impossible. Thus, infants might respond correctly based on an understanding of object permanence rather than an ability to calculate. To test this, Simon et al. presented Wynn's design but added two new conditions. In one, the outcome had the correct number of dolls, but the dolls' identity was changed. So infants might see one Ernie doll added to another Ernie doll behind a screen. Then the screen would be lowered to reveal an Ernie and an Elmo doll. The second new outcome had an incorrect number of dolls and incorrect identities. In the original conditions where physical and arithmetical correctness were confounded, 5-month-olds showed the same pattern of results reported by Wynn; they looked longer toward incorrect than toward correct outcomes. In contrast, infants did not look longer when the identities of the dolls were switched but the

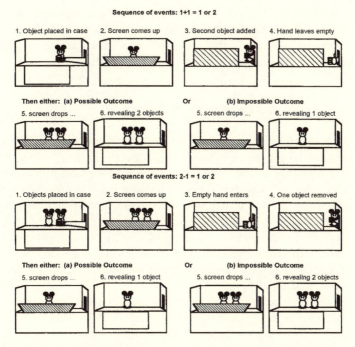

Sequence of events: 1+1 = 1 or 2

1. Object placed in case   2. Screen comes up   3. Second object added   4. Hand leaves empty

Then either: (a) Possible Outcome   Or   (b) Impossible Outcome

5. screen drops ...   6. revealing 2 objects   5. screen drops ...   6. revealing 1 object

Sequence of events: 2-1 = 1 or 2

1. Objects placed in case   2. Screen comes up   3. Empty hand enters   4. One object removed

Then either: (a) Possible Outcome   Or   (b) Impossible Outcome

5. screen drops ...   6. revealing 1 object   5. screen drops ...   6. revealing 2 objects

FIGURE 2.3 Sequence of events used in Wynn's (1992) addition condition. Reprinted with permission from Wynn, K. (1992). Addition and subtraction by human infants. *Nature*, 358, 749–50. Copyright 1992 *Nature*. Reprinted with permission of *Nature* and K. Wynn.

solution remained arithmetically correct. This indicated that, as Wynn had proposed, infants' responses were based on numerical rather than physical reasoning.

However, there is another possible basis for infants' responses. As Huttenlocher (1994) argued, infants could represent the problems in terms of overall amount rather than discrete number. In fact, this is what one would expect given Clearfield and Mix's (1999) finding that infants discriminate between quantities on the basis of overall amount.

A recent study provides direct evidence that overall amount forms the basis of infants' responses in this calculation task. Feigenson and Spelke (1998) used a procedure parallel to Wynn's (1992) but manipulated the size of the puppets to control for changes in total amount. For example, in the 1 + 1 problem, infants saw one small puppet placed behind a screen and then a second puppet of the same size placed behind the same screen. When the screen dropped, the infants saw either one large puppet (incorrect number but the same overall amount as the two small puppets) or two large puppets (correct number but incorrect amount). Infants attended to the display with the unexpected change in amount and the expected number rather than to the display with the unexpected number and the expected amount. This result parallels Clearfield and Mix's findings in the habituation procedure.

What Has Been Demonstrated in Infants

The studies described in this chapter provide clear evidence that infants are sensitive to the quantitative information in their environments—a far cry from what would have been predicted based on previous views of quantitative development. However, these new findings do not prove that infants have a sophisticated understanding of number, as some investigators have claimed. Although the evidence is quite strong for some abilities, such as discrimination of small sets, it is less conclusive for others. Moreover, even when evidence for a competence is well established, the basis for infants' responses is debatable. Let's briefly summarize the main findings.

The existing literature contains ample demonstrations that infants can discriminate between different set sizes. This is true for large sets that are highly discrepant, but it is also true for small sets that differ by one. This ability is present from birth (Antell & Keating, 1983) and is evident throughout infancy across a variety of experimental conditions. Infants react to changes in set size whether the sets are made up of heterogeneous items (Starkey et al., 1990), items that vary in size and type (Strauss & Curtis, 1981), items that are in motion (vanLoosbroek & Smitsman, 1990), or temporal sequences of events (Canfield & Smith, 1996; Wynn, 1996). The effects reported in these studies come from averaging looking times across infants and trials, so although these findings suggest that each individual can discriminate small sets, none demonstrates it directly. Still, this body of work offers convincing proof that infants are sensitive to quantitative information. The question is "What forms the basis of this sensitivity?".

As noted before, this sensitivity seems to be based on overall amount, at least for visual sets of objects (Clearfield & Mix, 1999). Such a starting point implies that infants' first ideas about quantity are not based on discrete number but rather that number and overall amount are united in an undifferentiated sense of quantity. Furthermore, because scanning edges and surfaces is a fundamental way infants can interpret visual scenes (Gibson, 1969), there is no need to posit a number-specific mechanism. Instead, quantitative knowledge could emerge as infants analyze the visual world via domain-general processes.

Evidence for infants' recognition of quantitative relations is considerably less compelling than that for discrimination. Preferential looking studies that have tested 6- to 8-month-olds' ability to abstract numerical equivalence across set types have resulted in an ambiguous set of findings with small effects in both directions of preference (Mix, Levine, & Huttenlocher, 1997; Moore et al., 1987; Starkey et al., 1990). There is also evidence suggesting that any real preference in these studies is driven by attention to rate and duration information (Mix et al., 1997). Direct evidence that infants detect equivalence relations is not obtained until infants reach 10 months of age (Cooper, 1984), and, as with other habituation studies, this is found only by averaging over infants and trials. Furthermore, infants' responses could have been based on differences in overall amount because Cooper's displays were not controlled to separate amount from number. Experiments showing that 14- to 16-month-olds understand ordinal relations have also confounded number and amount (Cooper, 1984; Curtis & Strauss, reported in Strauss & Curtis, 1984). Moreover, further study is needed simply to replicate and extend these preliminary findings. Thus, at the present time, there is no solid evidence that infants can recognize any kind of numerical relation before 10 months of age and only scant evidence that they can do so for certain relations in later infancy.

Finally, several studies have tested whether infants react to an incorrect solution to a simple addition or subtraction problem. Indeed, infants as young as 5 months old do look longer on average when an incorrect solution is shown, suggesting that they understand something about the nature of numerical transformations (Simon et al., 1995; Wynn, 1992). However, as in the number discrimination studies, this understanding may be based on attention to overall mass rather than discrete number (Feigensen & Spelke, 1998).

Do Infants Have "True" Number Concepts?

Several researchers have interpreted infants' performance in the experiments reviewed here as evidence of sophisticated reasoning abilities that are based on exact representations of discrete number. Thus, Wynn (1992) concludes that "infants are able to calculate the precise results of simple arithmetical operations" and that this indicates "infants possess true numerical concepts" (p. 750). Similarly, Starkey (1992) claims that infants can enumerate sets by using either a symbolic tagging process or a one-to-one mapping that directly compares the numerosities of sets. In either case, an exact representation of number is needed.

In many ways, the question of whether infants possess "true number concepts" is more philosophical than empirical because it is not clear how one would define a true number concept. In fact, it is not obvious that such a point in development ever comes because humans' concepts are continually evolving. As Douglass (1925) put it, "there is no limit which may be set to the extension or perfection of a concept. It is never complete, and the bounds of development are limitless" (p. 445).

However, this claim is undermined by an even more basic problem. Specifically, there is no empirical evidence that infants can represent the exact number of discrete entities. Studies showing that infants use overall amount rather than number in habituation and calculation tasks involving visual objects (Clearfield & Mix, 1999; Feigenson & Spelke, 1998) suggest a different starting point altogether—one based on an initially undifferentiated sense of amount. One might argue that infants have exhibited "true number concepts" in tasks involving events (Canfield & Smith, 1996; Wynn, 1996). However, such arguments are limited by the need for additional research to confirm that infants' responses in these tasks are not based on rhythm or some other confounding variable.

Even if infants can represent event sequences as sets of discrete entities that vary in quantity, these representations might be inexact for small set sizes, just like adults' representations for large set sizes if they do not count (Huttenlocher, Levine, & Jordan, 1994). Recall that what has been found is a tendency, across infants and trials, to attend less to a particular numerosity and more to a different numerosity. Although this is an important discovery, it does not necessarily indicate use of exact representations. Instead, number might be represented only approximately, as a generalization gradient centered at the true numerosity.

We will reserve further discussion of these interpretive questions for chapter 4, where we can consider these arguments in light of the evidence from birth through preschool age. For now, we conclude that because looking paradigms are open to the alternative interpretations we described, they may not be sufficiently sensitive to permit assessment of the hypothesis that infants can represent small numbers and number transformations exactly. That is, it may not be possible to determine from differential looking times that infants use exact representations of number, even if they do so. Tasks that can be given to toddlers, where they indicate the exact answer by choosing between two arrays that differ by one, or by constructing a set with the proper number of objects, make it possible, at least in principle, to determine the accuracy of children's performance. Such studies are the focus of the next chapter, in which we discuss what is known about preschoolers' understanding of discrete number.

3

Quantification in Early Childhood

Before researchers began to investigate the quantitative abilities of infants, there was controversy over the development of quantitative concepts in early childhood. This started in reaction to Piaget's finding that young children fail to conserve number, behavior that he interpreted as an inability to comprehend fundamental number concepts. However, researchers in the 1960s and 1970s challenged this interpretation on several fronts. As noted previously, some argued that children actually *can* conserve when different experimental procedures are used (e.g., Braine, 1959). Disagreement about whether these new procedures measured the same underlying competence as Piaget's task consumed the quantitative development literature and initiated widespread debate about the distinction between competence and performance (see Sophian, 1997, for a discussion).

At its core, this controversy concerned whether young children were quantitatively competent. However, accepting Piaget's assertion that conservation was the defining attribute of quantitative competence, each side constructed its argument on the presence or absence of it. Even if preschoolers cannot use one-to-one correspondence to establish numerical equivalence in the face of irrelevant spatial transformations, they may not be quantitatively incompetent. If we view development in terms of a gradual acquisition and integration of ideas, rather than the emergence of one defining skill, then we see evidence of many important quantitative concepts in early childhood (Baroody, 1987).

In this chapter, we review research on three key numerical abilities in early childhood: (1) recognition of equivalence, (2) recognition of ordinal relations, and (3) calculation with discrete sets. All the studies we include address children's number concepts prior to mastery of conventional symbol systems. We reserve our discussion of counting system acquisition and number fact calculation for chapter 8, where we address the relation between early concepts and formal symbol systems.

Recognition of Equivalence between Sets

In the previous chapter, we found little evidence that infants recognize numerical equivalence. First, although several studies have shown that infants respond to changes in set size via habituation, only one study has reported that infants (at 10 months) detect equivalence when two sets are compared (i.e., Cooper, 1984). It is important to replicate this key finding to confirm this ability. However, even if infants can make quantitative comparisons these may be based on overall amount rather than discrete number (Clearfield & Mix, 1999; Feigenson & Spelke, 1998). Furthermore, differential looking time measures, like those used to test equivalence judgments in infants, cannot provide unambiguous evidence of exact representations of number. So even if infants can compare discrete sets, their comparisons may not be based on exact representations.

Clear evidence of numerical equivalence judgments can be obtained with tasks that require choosing or constructing an equivalent set. Using such measures, several studies have assessed children's understanding of cardinal equivalence. If claims that infants can detect numerical equivalence are true, then we would expect very young children to succeed on such tasks as soon as they can comprehend the task demands. However, whereas children do demonstrate equivalence judgments on production and choice tasks, the following review indicates this ability emerges after the age of 2 years and starts with approximate responding.

Gelman's (1972) "magic experiment" was one of the earliest choice tasks used to test equivalence judgments. In her procedure, 3- to 6-year-old children were taught that a set of either two or three toy mice was the "winner." Over several trials, the two sets of mice were covered and shuffled. After children pointed to the set that they thought was the winner (as in the Shell Game), the two sets were uncovered and children were given feedback on their choice. Once children reliably recognized the winner set when it was uncovered, a test trial was presented in which the winner set was surreptitiously altered. The transformation was either a numerically irrelevant change in the length or density of the array (spatial displacement) or an addition or subtraction that changed the number of mice. Gelman found that children still recognized the winner set despite changes in spatial arrangement; however, when the change involved addition or subtraction, children correctly responded that there was no winner.

A subsequent study used the same procedure but now the irrelevant transformations involved the homogeneity of the sets (Gelman & Tucker, 1975). In one experiment, children correctly ignored the replacement of one mouse in the winner set with a mouse of a different color. However, in a second experiment, when one mouse was replaced with a toy soldier, over half of the children failed to identify the winner. When Gelman and Tucker reversed the order of the transformation so that the toy soldier was replaced with a mouse, performance improved. However, children were still confused about the disappearance of the soldier and asked to inspect both sets first. These results indicate that by 3 years of age, most children can identify small sets despite number irrelevant transformations; however, children may be more sensitive to some changes than to others.

Huttenlocher, et al. (1994) obtained evidence of a similar ability using a production task. In their study, an experimenter placed a set of black disks in full view of the child and then covered the set with a box. The child's task was to produce an equivalent set of black disks. By 2 years 6 months of age, most children could match at least two items. The highest numerosities children could match increased with age so that by their fourth birthdays, nearly all children matched up to three items and about half matched up to four. These results, along with those of Gelman's magic experiments, demonstrate that young children can use cardinality to compare and produce small sets. However, these studies provided no evidence regarding the range of set types to which equivalence judgments can be applied or how this range might vary throughout development.

Our subsequent research has revealed significant growth in the range of numerical comparisons young children can make. Mix et al. (1996) established that children can recognize equivalence between identical sets earlier than they can recognize equivalence in highly disparate comparisons. This study was designed to test the auditory-visual numerical matching ability Starkey, Spelke, and Gelman (1990) attributed to infants. Recall that infants had looked longer at a set of objects when it matched a set of drumbeats in number (see chapter 2 for a detailed discussion of this procedure). Mix et al. tested auditory-visual matching in preschoolers by presenting a standard set and then asking children to indicate which of two choice cards showed a numerically equivalent row of dots. For the auditory-visual matching task, the standard sets were series of claps. For the visual-visual control task, the standard sets were rows of black disks. To parallel the memory demands of the auditory-visual task, these disks were left in full view of the child for a few seconds and then were covered with a box. At age 3 years, children performed at chance on the auditory-visual match, even though they performed significantly above chance when matching sets of disks to the choice cards. In contrast, 4-year-olds performed significantly above chance in both conditions. Thus, children recognize equivalence for some comparisons before others, depending on the features of the sets.

Mix (1999a, 1999b) further explored these effects in a series of studies that tested a range of variations in set type and presentation. Using the same matching procedure described before, Mix varied the contents and presentation of the standard sets to determine which features affected children's equivalence judgments. Figure 3.1 shows the various trial types. In addition to these visual object sets, there were also comparisons involving visual events (puppet jumps; light flashes). As in the other conditions, the child's task was to point to the card that showed an array of dots equal in number to the sequence of events (e.g., two jumps = two dots).

Figure 3.2 shows the age at which children's matching scores exceeded chance in each of these conditions. It appears that children gradually recognize equivalence across increasingly disparate comparisons, rather than generalizing all at once. Three-year-olds, the youngest children who performed above chance on the matching task, recognized equivalence for only the most literal match: black disks to black dots. By $3\frac{1}{2}$ years of age, children recognized equivalence between different homogeneous visual sets. These children also matched sequential and static sets that contained highly similar items. However, children did not recognize equivalence for comparisons involving heterogeneous object sets until $4\frac{1}{2}$ years of age. Further, children recognized equivalence for comparisons between dots and sequentially presented events (i.e., light flashes and puppet jumps) by 4 years of age. Thus, a gradual progression takes place between 3 and 4 years of age that begins with success on the most literal comparisons, extends to other comparisons involving dissimilar homogeneous sets, and finally encompasses comparisons involving heterogeneous sets.

Taken together, these studies provide evidence that preschoolers can represent and compare small sets. However, children do not immediately detect equivalence in all possible comparisons. Instead, early equivalence judgments are moderated by the degree of similarity between the sets being compared. Accurate equivalence judgments emerge at $2\frac{1}{2}$ years of age but only for literal comparisons between disks and disks. Not until 4 to $4\frac{1}{2}$ years of age can children abstract equivalence relations across sets of items that do not share surface features, such as sounds and dots.

Until now, we have assumed that children's responses in these equivalence tasks were based on discrete number. However, evidence that infants use overall amount to perform quantitative tasks forces us to re-

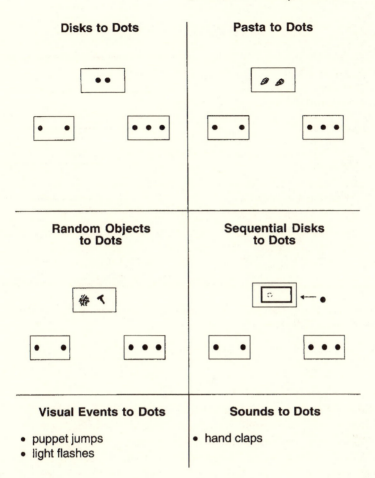

FIGURE 3.1 A graphic representation of the various trial types Mix (1999a; 1999b) has used.

consider this assumption. In fact, though we can conclude that individual children represented the quantities quite accurately, there is nothing built into the previous procedures to ensure that children represented number and not amount. However, Mix (in preparation) recently completed a matching study in which the sizes of the items were varied so that number and amount were separated. Children saw a standard set composed of two, three, or four squares. Their task was to identify the numerically equivalent set from among three choices. The squares in the three choice sets were the same size but either larger or smaller than squares in the standard set. Thus, the numerically equivalent set differed from the standard set in overall area. To see whether children matched on the basis of amount, one of the three choice sets

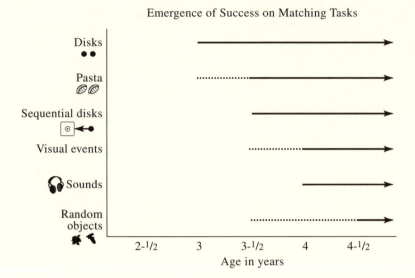

FIGURE 3.2 Shows the age at which children's matching scores exceeded chance in various conditions.

matched the standard in overall area but differed in number. The third choice set did not match the standard in either number or area. It was included to test whether children were guessing randomly.

Mix (in preperation) tested children from 2 years 6 months to 3 years 6 months of age. Across this age range, children chose the number match at greater than chance levels (45% vs. 33%) and more frequently than either the area match or the random choice (29% and 25%, respectively). Thus, children in this age range can respond on the basis of discrete number rather than amount. Because the children in previous numerical equivalence studies were at least 2 1/2 years old, it is likely that they, too, responded on the basis of number. Another key finding was that children who were not proficient counters still recognized numerical equivalence. In fact, children who did not know the meanings of even "one" and "two" still chose the numerical match more often than chance (42% vs. 33%). Thus, this ability emerges prior to acquisition of a conventional representation of number.

The preschool studies we reviewed indicate that children recognize equivalence much earlier than most children conserve number in Piaget's task. How is this possible? One reason might be differences in extra-numerical task demands. As we discussed previously, some investigators argued that children are confused by the questioning language and perceptual salience of the transformation in Piaget's task (e.g., Braine, 1959; Gelman, 1969). Neither Gelman's magic experiments nor our matching experiments fall prey to these criticisms. First, there can be no problem with the questioning language because these tasks are basically nonverbal. Second, rather than highlighting the transformation as Piaget did, both procedures deemphasized length and density changes by either performing them behind a screen or varying them randomly across trials. Thus, children might have revealed early conservation abilities in these less demanding tasks.

Another possibility is that children *can* use a one-to-one process to establish equivalence when small set sizes are involved. For example, children in Huttenlocher et al.'s (1994) matching task might have produced an equivalent set by laying out one disk for every disk that they represented in memory. Applying a one-to-one process such as this may be limited depending on how many items and one-to-one mappings a child can keep in memory. Of course, applying a one-to-one process is different from using the logic of one-to-one correspondence to conserve. Piaget was particularly interested in whether children knew that two sets that had been in one-to-one correspondence remained equivalent even when the physical correspondence was disrupted. He purposely used large sets so that this understanding could be tested separately from the ability to use counting or one-to-one correspondence to check equivalence. Because the equivalence tasks we reviewed used small sets, they may have tapped this latter ability.

Alternatively, these small number tasks might have allowed children to use a preconventional representation of cardinality to judge equivalence. That is, rather than using a one-to-one process (e.g., * * * = @ @ @ because *@*@*@), children could have compared the cardinal values of the sets (e.g., * * * = @ @ @ because 3 = 3). This approach would not require conventional counting skill because, as we shall see in chapter 7, children can represent up to four items nonverbally. Thus, conservation might emerge later than competence on the preschool equivalence tasks because the set sizes used by Piaget were too large to be represented nonverbally.

Recognition of Ordinal Relations

The tests of cardinal equivalence we described could be completed without any knowledge of relative magnitude. For example, one can know that three equals three without knowing that three is less than four. However, as discussed previously, numbers are defined in part by their relations to other numbers, and knowledge of these relations is required to comprehend the counting system and complex concepts such as decomposition (e.g., seven is equal to three plus four). Our review of the infant number literature revealed only scant evidence that infants are aware of ordinality. Interestingly, this awareness was evident late in infancy and several months after infants demonstrate an awareness of equivalence, suggesting that ordinal relations are more difficult to perceive.

We argued against claims that infants' responses in equivalence tasks were based on representations of exact number because the existing studies could not rule out the use of overall amount or approximate representations of discrete number. The same arguments apply to the data on ordinal awareness in infants. However, production or choice tasks make it possible to test precise ordinal judgments in slightly older children. We turn to such studies next.

The simplest ordinal task is identifying which of two amounts is more than the other. Bullock and Gelman (1977) tested this ability in preschoolers using a variation of Gelman's (1969) magic experiments. They taught children to recognize either one mouse or two mice as "the winner" following Gelman's training procedure (see the previous section). At test, rather than altering one of the arrays, they presented two novel set sizes to see whether children would choose the same ordinal relation. For example, given the choice between three and four mice at test, would children taught that two mice is the winner select the larger of the two test sets? Starting at age 3 years, children did transfer the ordinal relation to the test situation but only when asked "Which is the best winner?" At 2½ years of age, children failed to transfer unless the original sets were available for inspection during the test phase. Nonetheless, these results demonstrate that preschoolers can detect ordinal relations.

As in the studies of numerical equivalence, we cannot know whether children's ordinal judgments were based on overall amount or discrete number. For example, Bullock and Gelman (1977) asked whether children could recognize that four mice were greater than three mice. However, because the mice were identical, children could have solved this problem in terms of overall amount of mouse. Brannon and Van de Walle (1999) addressed this confound with a version of Gelman's "winner" experiments in which the surface area of the items was varied. As before, 2- to 3-year-olds were taught to identify the larger or smaller of two sets in a series of training trials. However, the objects were varied so that the set with the greater number also had the greater amount only a third of the time. In the remaining trials, the larger numerical set was smaller in overall amount. Nonetheless, children generalized the ordinal relation to novel numerical comparisons above chance levels. Although Brannon and Van de Walle did not test conventional counting ability, children in the age range they tested usually are not able to represent these quantities conventionally. This indicates that, as for equivalence judgments, ordinal responses based on discrete number appear early in childhood—without conventional counting skills. However, as in Mix's (in preparation) study of equivalence, children performed far from ceiling on this task (60% correct, where 50% is chance). Thus, transferring ordinal relations appears to be an emerging skill in this age range.

Although an understanding of ordinal relations emerges early in childhood, it takes some time for children to progress beyond simple "more than or less than" judgments. Fischer and Beckey (1990) tested increasingly complicated ordinal judgments in a sample of kindergarten children and found that, whereas nearly all the children they tested could correctly order two sets, only 23% correctly ordered four sets.

There is a striking parallel in the age of emergence for equivalence and ordinal judgments in childhood. Both skills appear between 2 and 3 years of age. Given the lack of proof of these notions in infancy, one might assume that they emerge simultaneously in early childhood. However, this conclusion is at odds with previous reports that ordination precedes cardination when within-subject comparisons are made (Brainerd 1973a, 1973b; Brainerd & Fraser, 1975; Siegel, 1974). Part of this discrepancy reflects differences in operational definition. For example, Brainerd's cardination task required children to compare two sets via one-to-one correspondence. He presented two picture cards with rows of dots and told children to determine whether the sets were equivalent without counting. Because the sets were too large to represent nonverbally, the only remaining strategy would be one-to-one correspondence. This definition of cardination is quite different from the one we have used in reference to early equivalence judgments (i.e., *** = @@@ because 3 = 3).

However, Brainerd and Fraser (1975) found that ordination also preceded children's ability to group sets based on cardinality. Their "number-as-class" task required 5- and 6-year-olds to sort piles of cards with different sets into groups that shared the same cardinal value. This is closer to the cardinal equivalence tasks we discussed earlier. Consistent with our review, competence on Brainerd's number-as-class task was evident before competence on his one-to-one cardination task. Yet it still emerged after children could arrange three clay balls according to weight or arrange three sticks according to length, lending support to the idea that ordination develops first. Similarly, Siegel (1974) found that 3½-year-olds were better at judging which of two sets had more items than they were at matching equivalent sets in a forced choice task. How is this possible when our review of the preschool literature indicated no such developmental ordering?

Differences in the set sizes used across experiments can account for this discrepancy. Both Brainerd and Siegel used sets too large for children to represent nonverbally. In the number-as-class task, children had to sort groups of four and six items. The sets in Siegel's matching task ranged from one to nine items. Most of these sets would be too large to represent cardinally without counting, so it would be impossible for children to detect equivalence before they had acquired conventional skills (unless the foils were highly discrepant in amount as well). In contrast, the small sets used in the preschool equivalence studies were within the range of a nonverbal representation. Thus, it is at least possible that children compared the cardinal values of the sets. Set size differences can also explain why children who failed Brainerd's tasks were older than those who succeeded in the preschool equivalence studies we reviewed earlier (e.g., Gelman, 1969; Huttenlocher et al., 1994; Mix, 1999a, 1999b).

To summarize, several studies have demonstrated that preschoolers can recognize the most basic ordinal relation, one set being greater than another (Bullock & Gelman, 1977; Siegel, 1974). Under certain circumstances, even 2-year-olds recognize simple ordinal relations (Brannon & Van de Walle, 1999; Bullock & Gelman, 1977). However, this may be a new development, given the lack of evidence that infants detect ordinality (see chapter 2). By 5 years of age, children can deal with complex ordinal relations in which more than two amounts are compared (Brainerd, 1973a; Fischer & Beckey, 1990). Thus, the overall pattern for recognition of ordinal relations parallels that for equivalence relations: it emerges in the preschool age range and gradually extends to increasingly complex comparisons.

Calculation: Understanding the Results of Numerical Transformations

In chapter 2, we reviewed evidence of calculation by 5- to 10-month-olds. Several studies reported that when shown simple addition and subtraction problems with sets of objects, infants looked significantly longer toward incorrect solutions than they did toward correct solutions. This indicates some understanding of quantitative transformations; however, this understanding is limited to problems involving very small sets (e.g., $1 + 1 = 2$) and may be based on changes in amount rather than on changes in number (Feigensen & Spelke, 1998). Nonetheless, it has been argued that these studies prove infants are "innately endowed" with arithmetical abilities and "true" number concepts. If so, and children have possessed exact numerical skills since infancy, then they should be able to produce correct calculation solutions reliably. However, studies of calculation in early childhood that used production tasks have not supported this prediction. Instead, precise calculation ability emerges after $2\frac{1}{2}$ years of age and continues to improve over the preschool age range.

Key evidence comes from a series of calculation studies with preschool children (Huttenlocher et al., 1994; Jordan, Huttenlocher, &

Levine, 1994; Levine, Jordan, & Huttenlocher, 1992). The problems were presented nonverbally by showing a set of objects and then hiding it under a box. Then, objects were either added to or removed from the hidden set, but the outcome could not be seen. The child's task was to indicate how many items were in the resultant array by either constructing an equivalent set of objects or pointing to a picture of an equivalent set. Children successfully solve these nonverbal problems at least one to two years earlier than they achieve comparable success on either verbal story problems or number fact problems (Levine et al., 1992).

When the youngest age limits were explored, nonverbal calculation ability first appeared in the 2- to 3-year-old age period (Huttenlocher et al., 1994). Although children between 2 and $2\frac{1}{2}$ years of age did not reliably produce correct solutions, their responses were not random—they varied around the correct solution. Starting at 2 years 6 months, they began to produce correct solutions to small number problems, such as $1 + 1 = 2$. By 3 years 6 months of age, the majority of children reliably solved these small number problems, and by the end of the third year, most children reliably solved slightly higher numerosity problems (e.g., $1 + 2$, $3 - 1$, $3 - 2$, etc.). Thus, when children begin to calculate, their responses shift from approximations of the correct solutions to consistently correct exact solutions.

Other calculation studies using active responses such as production or choice have reported competence in younger children than Huttenlocher et al. (1994). However, methodological problems with these studies raise questions about these claims. Sophian and Adams (1987) tested calculation in toddlers by presenting two sets of objects, covering them, and then transforming one of the sets behind the cover. Children were shown the transformation but could not see the resulting set. The test assessed whether the child would know which set was larger and choose it for himself. The authors claimed that children from 14 to 28 months calculated reliably in this task. However, this claim was not clearly supported. First, the authors assumed that children would choose the larger set if they knew the number of objects. However, on a baseline task with no transformations, children at 24 months did not reliably choose the set with more (two) items. Second, children up to 24 months tended to choose whichever set the experimenter manipulated, regardless of whether items were added or taken away and regardless of whether the resultant set was larger or smaller. Because the transformed set was often larger, consistently choosing the transformed set would falsely indicate an ability to calculate. One problem type avoided this confound by starting with unequal sets such that even when an object was added, the transformed set remained the smaller of the two. However, even the oldest subjects (28-month-olds) performed only slightly above chance on this problem (.60). Thus, this study does not provide conclusive evidence of calculation in children under 3 years. In fact, when Cooper (1984) used a similar method, he determined that 2-year-olds do not understand that the initial numerosity of a set is important for predicting the effect of the addition or subtraction of terms to that set.

In another test of calculation in toddlerhood, Starkey (1992) had children place a set of balls one at a time in an opaque box and then watch as balls were added or removed from the hidden set. Following the transformation, the child was told to remove all of the balls. Starkey reasoned that if children could calculate, the number of reaches would equal the resulting number of balls. To prevent children from feeling all the balls as they reached in, the entire set was secretly removed after the transformation and replaced one by one before each reach. However, this procedure creates a different problem. That is, children might *stop* reaching if they could determine by touch that there were no other objects in the box to be removed.

As Huttenlocher et al. (1994) argued, the data from Starkey's calculation task provide grounds to worry that touch cues (i.e., discovering that no other objects are present during a reach) led to score inflation. The calculation task was given to children from 18 months to 4 years of age. Across age, problems were easier when the answer was smaller, even when the same terms were involved. For example, two problems were presented that required children to represent four hidden objects: "4 – 3"and "4 – 1." These problems both involve the same additive relation (i.e., 1 + 3 = 4), so there is no apriori reason to think that one would be easier than the other. However, children had 64% correct for the problem "4 – 3," whereas they had only 14% correct for the problem "4 – 1." Such a result would be puzzling if children were calculating. However, it would be expected if children were using touch cues because such a strategy would bias children to stop at one reach.

Starkey's results showed that subjects did very well on the easiest calculation problems, 1 + 1 and 2 – 1, by 24 months. Given the problems with his procedure, the question arises of whether children's high scores could reflect use of touch as a cue together with approximate number abilities. Suppose children note that the initial array has some items but not the exact number and that, further, they note the direction but not the exact number of items involved in the transformation. For 1 + 1, they should expect more than one item in the final array and therefore might not use the cue from touch on the first reach. Having no further expectations, they might rely on touch on the second reach, leading to the correct answer. For 2 – 1, they should not expect more than one item in the final array and hence might use the cue from touch on the first reach, leading to the correct answer.

In summary, several studies have evaluated calculation ability in early childhood. Although some have reported that children can calculate with precision by 14 to 18 months of age, methodological problems leave open the possibility of alternative interpretations. The remaining studies indicate that precise calculation ability emerges between 2 and 3 years of age and continues to improve during the preschool period. Of course, this is still much earlier than children learn to calculate using conventional methods.

We cannot say with certainty that children's calculations in these studies were based on discrete number because experiments that separate number and amount in a calculation task have not been carried out. Because the items in Huttenlocher et al.'s (1994) calculation problems were identical, it is possible that children represented the overall amount in the resulting arrays and then produced sets that matched this representation in amount. However, findings of numerical responding in 2- to 3-year-olds on equivalence and ordinality tasks argue against this interpretation (Brannon & Van de Walle, 1999; Mix, in preparation). That is, if children this age can represent discrete number in these other tasks, there is reason to think that they do the same on the calculation task.

What Has Been Demonstrated in Preschoolers

The review presented in this chapter reveals that rather than being numerically incompetent, preschool children demonstrate many quantitative skills. They can judge equivalence between small sets (Gelman, 1969; Huttenlocher et al., 1994; Mix; 1999a; 1999b). This ability is initially limited to literal comparisons but gradually generalizes to a range of increasingly abstract comparisons by 4 to 4½ years of age (Mix, 1999a, 1999b; Mix et al., 1996). Preschoolers can also recognize ordinal relations, at least for simple comparisons between two sets. By kindergarten, children can perform more complex orderings among multiple sets. Finally, there is reliable evidence that preschool children can calculate. As with the understanding of equivalence and ordinality, calculation first emerges for the simplest problems involving small sets and later extends to more difficult problems involving larger sets. Notably, exact calculation is preceded by approximate, nonrandom responding.

The age of emergence is strikingly similar for the skills we reviewed. In all three cases—equivalence, ordination, and cardination—the ability to respond exactly first appears around 2½ years of age. Thus, the emergence of an exact representation of number might underlie advances across a range of numerical abilities. As Huttenlocher et al. (1994) proposed, this may be linked to the emergence of symbolic thought more generally. At the same time children display evidence of exact numerical representations, they also exhibit a variety of symbolic activities. Their play comes to involve the use of substitute objects and activities to "stand for" real objects and activities (e.g., McCune-Nicolich, 1981). They also become able to use physical models to provide information about actual situations. DeLoache (1987, 1991) found that the ability to infer the location of an actual toy in a room from watching a model toy being hidden in a model room appeared between 2½ and 3 years of age (the ability to use a picture as a representation of an actual spatial layout appeared somewhat earlier, by 2½ years). The co-occurence of these attainments might mean that early childhood advances in number concept development are linked to the development of other symbolic processes (but not conventional symbols) that arise in the 2- to 3-year- old age period.

Finally, let us return briefly to the relation between Piaget's work and the studies that have been published since then. Although the general idea that preschoolers lack numerical ability is disproved by subsequent studies, the developmental pathway described by Piaget (1941/1965) is still consistent with these findings. Piaget argued that ordination and cardination developed in separate but parallel sequences that gradually became coordinated. This process of coordination culminated in a mature concept of number that was reflected in performance on the number conservation task. The overall pattern reflected in our review is still consistent with this account. The main difference between Piaget's view and later research seems to be in the emphasis on conservation. Piaget recognized that cardination and ordination skills appeared prior to conservation, but he did not attach much significance to this. In contrast, subsequent research has highlighted the conceptual power that these understandings carry in their own right (e.g., Gelman, 1969).

Now that we have reviewed the developmental changes that occur in infancy and early childhood, we may consider the transition between these age periods. In chapter 4, we turn our attention to the different ways this transition can be characterized and the extent to which each characterization is supported empirically.

4

Quantification of Discrete Sets: A Synthesis

Over the past 20 years, a major research agenda has been to outline the competencies antecedent to acquisition of conventional mathematics skills. As the preceding chapters illustrate, this research has revealed an impressive range of abilities. Prior to mastering conventional skills, children can represent quantities, recognize equivalence, solve simple calculation problems, and transfer ordinal relations. But how do these abilities develop? What are their origins and how do they change?

When the focus is on the earliest point that a competence can be demonstrated, it is tempting to conclude that not much changes between infancy and acquisition of conventional skills. After all, infants have responded in ways that suggest an awareness of quantitative relations from an early age, sometimes within hours after birth. Thus, some believe that the crucial numerical principles are "wired in" (e.g., Gallistel & Gelman, 1992; Wynn, 1997). In this view, the main accomplishment of early childhood is mapping a conventional verbal system onto the nonverbal system. However, when one considers development across the entire infancy and early childhood period, a different picture emerges in which numerical skills gradually unfold and significantly change *throughout* the first years of life. In this chapter, we examine these changes and discuss possible explanations for them.

Let's begin by considering the big picture that emerges from the literature reviews of chapters 2 and 3. As figure 4.1 shows, sensitivity to quantity is evident virtually from birth. In fact, the ability to discriminate between small visual sets is probably the most robust, consistent,

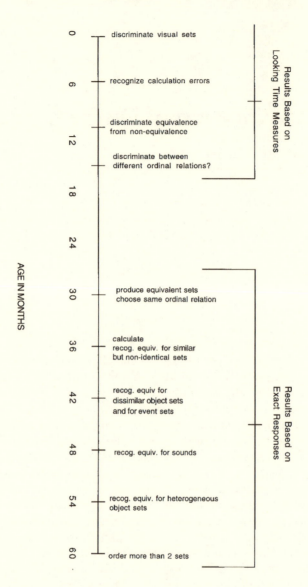

FIGURE 4.1 Timeline summarizing quantitiative development from birth to school age.

and well-documented finding in the infant literature. There is no reason to doubt that infants can do it. By 5 months, the youngest age tested, infants demonstrate rudimentary calculation skills. There is preliminary evidence that, somewhat later in infancy, quantitative relations, such as equality and ordinality, are recognized.

As we argued in chapter 2, though these findings are important, they do not necessarily support claims of exact numerical representations and reasoning in infancy. First, all of the reported effects are based on looking times averaged across infants and trials. Thus, apparent exact representations in individual infants could actually be the combination of many inexact representations. Second, infants seem to use overall amount rather than number to respond in habituation and calculation tasks. So we have reason to question whether infants can represent discrete number at all.

A major shift takes place at the start of early childhood in the type of tasks that children can do and thus the kind of experimental evidence obtained (see figure 4.1). Specifically, not until almost 3 years of age can children perform tasks that require an exact numerical response (e.g., choosing or producing a particular set). This turning point is critical because it is the first time that an exact representation of number is clearly evident in individual children.

The first skills to be demonstrated in exact response tasks are recognition of equivalence and ordinality between $2\frac{1}{2}$ and 3 years of age. A little later, children demonstrate the ability to calculate using a production task, initially limited to low numerosity problems but gradually extending to larger numerosity problems. For several years after exact responses are obtained in these tasks, children's performance continues to improve by extending to more complex and abstract situations. Around age 3, children start to recognize equivalence for sets that do not look exactly alike. Recall that Mix (1999a, 1999b) found 3-year-olds recognized equivalence between black disks and black dots. This comparison between three-dimensional objects and two-dimensional symbols is slightly more abstract than the literal identity match that Huttenlocher et al. (1994) found $2\frac{1}{2}$-year-olds could make. Between 3 and 5 years of age, children start to recognize equivalence between heterogeneous objects and dots (Mix, 1999a), visual event sets and dots (Mix, 1999b), and finally between sounds and dots (Mix et al., 1996). Thus, the range of conditions under which children can recognize equivalence increases during this period.

Children also improve on ordinality tasks. Specifically, 3- and 4-year-olds can transfer an ordinal relation even when the training standard was hidden, unlike $2\frac{1}{2}$-year-olds, who needed to inspect it in order to transfer their response to different numerosities (Bullock & Gelman, 1977). The ability to order more than two sets was not evident until much later, at kindergarten age and beyond (e.g., Fischer & Beckey, 1990). Thus, although exact responding in quantitative tasks emerges between $2\frac{1}{2}$ and 3 years of age, improvement and extension of these skills is evident throughout the preschool period.

The shift in methodology between infancy and preschool age leaves a gap in our knowledge about quantitative development between 16 and 30 months of age. The few studies that have tested exact number concepts in toddlers provide limited information because of methodological flaws (see chapter 3 for a discussion). Therefore, it is currently unclear what subtle changes might occur in the late infancy period and how these would relate to early childhood abilities. To gain a complete picture of early quantitative development, further research with toddlers is needed. These studies might reveal few significant changes, in which case the first accomplishments of early childhood would signal an abrupt transition. Alternatively, research with toddlers might reveal that exact responding emerges slowly between 16 and 30 months as part of a more gradual transition between infancy and early childhood.

A key finding from the preschool literature provides a hint about what might be happening in the toddler period. Huttenlocher et al. (1994) found that although 24- to 30-month-olds did not produce correct solutions to calculation problems, their responses were not random. Instead, the number of disks they laid out varied systematically with the number of disks in the correct solution. For example, when the correct answer was three disks, these children tended to respond with two, three, or four disks. This finding is consistent with the use of an approximate representation of quantity in early childhood, which suggests a continuity with the kind of competence infants demonstrate.

In summary, the big picture reveals a pattern of steady growth in quantitative understanding from birth to school age. These early emerging skills are hardly evidence of full-blown number concepts. In fact, the continual changes observed throughout this age range and beyond preclude any declaration of full-blown concepts. The extent of development occurring even in the preconventional period is remarkable. It suggests that preverbal number concepts are not a fully functioning innate endowment that need only be mapped onto the conventional verbal system. Rather, significant changes occur at the preverbal level itself.

Now that we have established the abilities demonstrated across the infancy and early childhood period, let's consider possible explanations for the developmental pattern itself. Three main changes are taking place with age: (1) the level of accuracy and precision that can be demonstrated empirically improves; (2) the set size that can be handled increases; and (3) the range of abstraction increases.

Accuracy and Precision

One of the most striking differences between the performance of infants and preschoolers in quantitative tasks is the degree of accuracy and precision in individual responses. As we noted, infant data consist of averages taken across the group. Effects in these studies are generally small because of variability in the data. In contrast, preschool children can perform tasks that require an exact response. Although there is still variability within age groups, evidence of a skill is more clear-cut, particularly in the individual child. We discuss four scenarios that might account for this discrepancy. In the first two, infants use essentially the same mechanism to represent quantity as young children use, but they do not apply it the same way. In the other two scenarios, the mechanism that infants use is different from the mechanism that children use.

Same Discrete Number Representation—Noisy Data

One possibility is that infants and young children are processing quantitative information essentially the same way, but infants appear to be different because they are often inattentive, sleepy, or fussy. Thus, both infants and children could represent exact number via the same preverbal mechanism, but infants' performance would not necessarily reflect this precision because of noise in their responses. For example, if babies aren't paying close attention to the habituation trials in a number discrimination experiment, they might not look longer on the dishabituation trials. In this scenario, the main change between infancy and early childhood would be an increase in attention and stamina that would allow numerical ability to be demonstrated in increasingly demanding tasks.

However, the noisy data explanation breaks down when we consider the transition from infancy to early childhood. In particular, there is no way to account for the inexact but nonrandom performance of 2-year-olds in Huttenlocher et al.'s (1994) calculation task. Recall that prior to accurately solving nonverbal calculation tasks, children produced approximate responses. This was true even though they were not sleepy or fussy. If infants use an exact mechanism to represent number that is not consistently tapped because of their inattention, we should see a radical shift once children can perform tasks that require exact responding. That is, as soon as toddlers can attend to the nonverbal calculation task, they should reveal this exact mechanism with accurate responses. However, as we noted, that is not the case. Instead, the youngest children who can complete the nonverbal calculation task produce responses that only *cluster around* the correct solution (Huttenlocher et al., 1994). This suggests that their responses are based on an approximation of the resulting quantity.

Same Discrete Number Representation—Implicit versus Explicit

A second possibility is that infants and young children use the same mechanism to process quantitative information, but infants lack conscious access to either the information or the process. Thus, when infants habituate to a certain set size, they make no judgment of numerical equivalence. Instead, they gradually stop responding to the same information repetitively. In this view, infants could not respond in tasks that require explicit knowledge (e.g., a forced choice task) because they could not intentionally apply the mechanism to enumerate sets. This is the possibility raised by Gelman and Brenneman (1994) who argue that although infants may possess innate knowledge of numerical principles, they lack access to this knowledge. Instead, the principles are represented implicitly within the structure of the information-processing mechanisms that assimilate and direct the infants' actions. However, this information presumably becomes explicit by early childhood when children first succeed at forced choice and production tasks. In this view, the main change between infancy and early childhood would be the transition from implicit to explicit access to numerical knowledge.

Again, if we assume that both infants and young children represent discrete number, then this explanation cannot account for the approximate responses of 2-year-olds in Huttenlocher et al.'s (1994) nonverbal calculation task. If infants can represent exact quantities but cannot demonstrate this ability in explicit tasks, then once children can complete explicit tasks, their responses should be precisely accurate. However, the data do not support this prediction. Even though 2-year-olds clearly understood the demands of the nonverbal calculation task and produced sets in response to the problem, they did not generate a precise response. Instead, they produced sets that approximated the correct solution, indicating that they were not guessing. This should not happen if the ability to represent exact quantities is present from infancy.

Of course, the issue of implicit versus explicit knowledge is separate from the issue of exact versus approximate representation. We cannot rule out the possibility that early quantitative knowledge is implicit, only that implicit knowledge would not mask the use of an exact mechanism. It is possible, at least in principle, that infants are using an *approximate* mechanism for discrete number that is initially implicit. Alternatively, infants and young children may represent quantities as amounts, but infants may not have explicit access to these representations. This account would imply that a great deal changes between infancy and early childhood—both the process itself and the child's access to it.

Different Representations—Discrete But Inexact

A third possibility is that infants can represent small discrete quantities but not by using an exact mechanism like that demonstrated in children. Instead, these representations might be inexact for small set sizes just as adults' representations are for large set sizes if they do not count (Gallistel & Gelman, 1992; Huttenlocher et al., 1994). Thus, an array of three might be represented as three or as two or four. Consider how such a mechanism could lead the results reported in habituation experiments. When an infant is presented with an array of a particular size (even a very small one), number might be represented as a generalization gradient centered at the true numerosity. This pattern of responses would be similar to that observed in number experiments with animals (e.g., Platt & Johnson, 1971) (see figure 4.2). Thus, the habituation arising over a series of trials would occur not only to the true numerosity, but also, to a lesser extent, to surrounding numerosities. When the new number is presented on the dishabituation trial, it also might be represented as a generalization gradient centered at the true numerosity. Within a particular infant on a particular set of trials, these gradients might overlap. Longer looking times would occur when the gradients are sufficiently distinct from one another—that is, on those dishabituation trials where the representation of the new number differs enough from the representation formed on the habituation trials to be discriminable.

If infants use approximations of discrete quantity, the main accomplishment of early childhood would be the development of precise representations that can be used in conventional mathematics problems. This might happen if the mechanism that produces approximate representations is replaced or evolves into a more exact representation. For example, when children learn to count, the count words might map onto the central tendencies of the generalization gradients. This process would provide a translation from the approximations of the true quantity into precise numbers. A similar translation process might occur nonverbally if children acquire a one-to one symbolic representation prior to mastering the count word tags. Or, the representation might never become truly precise, even in early childhood. Instead, the generalization gradients around each true numerosity might narrow gradually until the

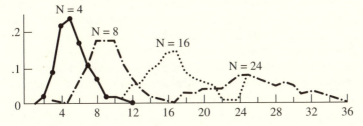

FIGURE 4.2 Number of lever presses as a function of the desired number (based on Platt and Johnson, 1971). Platt, J. R. and Johnson, D. M. (1971). Localization of position within a homogenous behavior chain: Effects of error contingencies. *Learning and Motivation*, 2, 386–414. Reprinted with permission from Academic Press.

resulting representations approach exactness. This of course would become exact when conventional symbols are learned, but in the age range that children perform exact matching and production tasks without mastery of conventional skills, it is possible that they operate with a very accurate approximate mechanism. The use of an approximate mechanism in infancy is consistent with what is known about the emergence of exact responding in nonverbal calculation—namely that this is preceded by a period of responding *around* the correct answer. Thus, this third scenario would draw a tenuous continuity between the literatures on infant and preschool number acquisition.

Different Representation—Continuous versus Discrete

A fourth possibility is that infants represent quantity with an approximate mechanism that is based on continuous amount rather than discrete number (Clearfield & Mix, 1999; Huttenlocher, 1994). Thus, rather than attending to the number of individual items and generating a representation based on a one-to-one mapping of the entire set (although an inexact mapping), babies might attend not to the individual items but to the overall amount in mass, area, and so forth that tends to covary with number. Inexactness would be virtually guaranteed in such a representation because it is only possible to estimate continuous amount to some degree of precision. In this view the main developmental change would involve learning to quantify discrete sets independent of the size or mass of each item.

As we noted, several investigators have varied the size of items used in their visual displays in an attempt to rule out this possibility (e.g., Starkey et al., 1990; Strauss & Curtis, 1981). However, these studies do not provide details about the relative area and contour length of items in their displays, so it is unclear whether systematic comparisons were made (e.g., equal area/different number vs. unequal area/same number). Furthermore, it is not clear how these investigators ensured that the differences in continuous amount were discriminable. Discriminable differences in continuous quantity are more likely between sets that differ in number than between sets of the same number, unless these differences are minimized in the former case and exaggerated in the latter. In other words, unless investigators intentionally made number sets discriminably different in size, area, contour length, and so on and ensured that the trials that differed in number were not discriminably different in terms of continuous quantity, the possibility that infants use continuous amount instead of discrete quantity has not been ruled out. Indeed several studies have shown that, under such conditions, infants do view quantities in terms of continuous amount (Clearfield & Mix, 1999, 2000; Feigenson & Spelke, 1998). The definitive answer to this question awaits further research. Like the approximate but discrete scenario, this possibility also aligns well with the preschool literature. If infants respond to continuous quantity rather than discrete quantity, then their representations would be inherently inexact. This inexactness would connect with the initially imprecise responses of young children in the nonverbal calculation task (Huttenlocher et al., 1994).

Which Interpretation Is Correct?

Although the approximate responses produced by 2-year-olds in Huttenlocher et al.'s (1994) nonverbal calculation task do not seem consistent with an exact response in infancy, they are only one piece of the puzzle. More information about quantitative skills in toddlers is needed to determine whether this finding is robust across tasks. In the meantime, looking paradigms are probably not sensitive enough to assess whether infants can represent small numbers and number transformations exactly. Even if infants use exact representations, evidence based on differential looking times cannot demonstrate that this, and not approximate representations, underlies infants' performance. Finally, if we assume that infants use an approximate mechanism, this may be based on continuous rather than discrete quantity (Clearfield & Mix, 1999; Feigensen & Spelke, 1998).

One thing is certain—until more is known, strong claims of precise, counting-like operations in infancy are premature. In the meantime, we propose a more conservative interpretation in which infants start out with a sensitivity to approximate quantity probably based on overall amount. Over toddlerhood, this representation is replaced or augmented by one based on discrete number. By preschool age, children use this representation to perform tasks that require explicit, exact responses. Not long after, conventional symbols are acquired and mapped onto these discrete, preverbal representations.

Clearly, more research is needed to elucidate certain aspects of this account. For example, how can children represent discrete number preconventionally? What causes this representation to emerge? When and how do children differentiate between continuous and discrete quantification? Although we do not have all the answers, identifying and acknowledging the changes that occur is an important first step because it leads to these productive questions and opens up new lines of inquiry that can address them.

Set Size

A second major change that is apparent when development across infancy and early childhood is examined is an increase in the set size that can be processed. Infants are able to deal with comparisons between only the smallest of sets. For example, infants can discriminate two dots from three dots, but not four from six (Starkey & Cooper, 1980). Similarly, infant calculation has been shown in problems involving only very small quantities (e.g., 1 + 1 = 2) (Wynn, 1994). Since there is only weak evidence that infants can discriminate three from four (Strauss & Curtis, 1981), there is no reason to attribute a sense of threeness to them. In fact, infants' responses on nearly all the tasks they have performed could be explained by an ability to detect "two" from "not two." This would connect with the performance of very young children that also appears to be limited to sets of one and two. When preschoolers begin matching at around 2½ years old, they can do so with any degree of accuracy only for sets of one and two (Huttenlocher et al., 1994). Slightly older children can match sets of three with over 50% accuracy, but not until 3 years 9 months of age can they match sets of four. By the time they turn 4 years old, most children still cannot reliably match sets of five.

This progression is also seen in nonverbal calculation ability (Huttenlocher et al., 1994). When 3-year-olds begin to calculate precisely, they first succeed on problems with only the smallest total numerosity (i.e., 1 + 1 = 2; 2 − 1 = 1). Children who are several months older are reasonably accurate on problems involving slightly larger numerosities (i.e., 1 + 2 = 3). By the time children turn 4 years old, they begin to deal with problems involving four or more items. Thus, in both equivalence judgments and calculation, the set sizes that can be represented and transformed increase over development. However, this might top out at four or five items around the time when children master conventional counting.

Why would this change occur? One possibility is that improvements in memory over this age range would allow children to keep track of more items at a time. For example, to perform the nonverbal calculation task, children need to remember how many items are under the cover during the transformation. The memory demands may increase with set size depending on the way the cardinal value of the set is represented (see chapter 7 for a discussion). If so, then as children improve their memory capabilities in general, their performance on numerical tasks would improve.

Another possibility is that the way number is processed and represented changes to allow greater precision with larger sets. For example, if quantity is represented continuously at first (as in the fourth scenario above), smaller quantities would be easier to discriminate because they would involve the largest discrepancies in amount. For example, comparing one item with two items of the same size is tantamount to comparing one amount with its double. As set size increases, the proportional difference in amount decreases, so comparing three items with four items via a continuous mechanism would be more difficult than two versus three. Children may become able to discriminate larger sets once this process has been replaced with a process that can handle discrete number.

The changes in set size limits observed in infancy and early childhood have an important theoretical implication. Previous researchers have noted a similarity between the set sizes that adults can estimate rapidly, or subitize, and the set sizes that infants can discriminate: both are less than five items. This similarity has led some to suggest that subitizing is an innate ability that humans share with other animals (e.g., Trick & Pylyshyn, 1994). However, the patterns just described tell a different story. Whereas adults can subitize at least five items, young children only gradually develop the ability to deal with exact numbers larger than two. This development indicates that rapid enumeration of sets with five items or fewer is not a given. If adult subitizing really is rooted in infant sensitivity to number, then the subitizing process itself must undergo significant development in the first few years. On the other hand, subitizing might be unrelated to the process underlying infants' behavior. No real empirical link connects these two phenomena except the similarity in set size, and as we have seen a close examination of the data on set size limits does not reveal such a strong similarity, at least not early on.

Abstraction

A third change that takes place in preverbal quantitative development is in the degree of abstraction with which number concepts are applied. This turns out to be a rather complex issue because infants respond to number in a variety of contexts. For example, infants can discriminate two jumps from three jumps (Wynn, 1996). They can also discriminate between set sizes for heterogeneous arrays of objects (Starkey et al., 1990). Therefore, on the face of it, it seems that infants' concepts of number are quite abstract—indeed, this has been the claim (Starkey et al., 1990; Wynn, 1996).

However, this conclusion does not match what is happening in preschool. Instead, when all the studies that have involved comparing two sets are considered, there appears to be a gradual increase in abstraction. Starting at age 2 years, children can recognize equivalence between identical sets of objects—black disks to black disks (Huttenlocher et al., 1994). However, Mix (1999b) found that children could not compare a set of objects to a picture of the same objects until 3 years of age. Between 3 and 5 years of age, children gradually extend to comparisons involving dissimilar homogeneous and eventually heterogeneous object sets (Mix, 1999b). Also in this age range, children slowly generalize to event sets, such as puppet jumps (Mix, 1999a).

This pattern probably does not reflect representational change because whatever process children use to enumerate disks should apply to any set of objects. Instead, children apparently fail to see the numerical relation between sets of objects that differ in appearance. This suggests an interesting possibility. There may be a period when children can detect the numerosity of a particular set without seeing numerosity as the basis for categorization (Mix, 1999b).

This possibility has not been raised previously for number concept development. However, it is consistent with work on the development of other concepts, such as color (Smith, 1993; Sandhofer & Smith, 1999). This research has revealed that children can name different objects according to color before they can group items of the same color. Smith (1993) accounts for these findings by distinguishing between different senses of sameness. In one sense—what she calls "implicit sameness"—children generalize a response from one instance to the next. So a child might see something red, recognize that it is red, and perhaps even label it "red." The child could generate the same response across many instances without understanding that all red things are the same because they are the same color. In other words, similarity would be implied to an observer because the same color evokes the same response. However, this would not mean that the child sees all red things as members of a common equivalence class.

This implicit sense of sameness might underlie early number processing. In habituation, infants might see a set of two and perceive twoness or some approximation of twoness, see another set of two and perceive twoness, and so forth. Over repeated exposures, infants would slowly respond less and less to this stimulation. They could do this without knowing that sets of two belong to the same class and that this class is different from the class of sets of three. Infant response to number in a variety of contexts might be considered a narrow type of abstraction, but certainly it is not what we mean when we talk about numerical abstraction in adults or older children. Adult abstraction requires a different sense of sameness in which the perceiver compares multiple sets and judges them to be the same or different along some dimension.

Smith (1993) refers to this as "explicit sameness" or recognizing similarity across instances via a comparison process. For color, this would involve seeing several red objects and grouping them *because* they are all red. Explicit sameness would allow children to abstract number across various contexts, to match even disparate sets on the basis of numerical equivalence. Given the extant findings, this ability seems to develop slowly, perhaps as children gain experience with classes of entities in the world.

Conclusions

In this chapter, we synthesized the major research findings on the development of discrete number concepts from infancy to early childhood. Instead of focusing on the earliest point when any kernel of competence can be demonstrated, this synthesis aims to flesh out a frequently ignored view—the view of what connects and distinguishes the abilities demonstrated across the infancy–early childhood age range. In many cases, this focus led to more questions than answers. However, we believe that these are the questions that should be asked if knowledge in this area is to be advanced.

5

Continuous Amount

Entities may be quantified in terms of either number or amount. Both modes of quantification frequently yield the same answer to a particular question because number tends to covary with amount. Thus, a pile of 36 apples has more apples and typically has more apple stuff than a pile containing 12 apples. However, quantification based on number can differ greatly from quantification based on amount if the items involved are radically different in size. For example, two sets may have the same number but differ markedly in total amount of substance (e.g., eight elephants vs. eight ants). Conversely, two sets may be the same in total amount but differ in number (e.g., one full chocolate bar vs. the twelve pieces into which it could be divided). For adults, the number of discrete elements in a set and the amount of substance in that set are clearly different notions. How does this understanding develop?

In previous chapters, we focused on the development of discrete number concepts because most developmental studies have tested children's responses to discrete sets. This is partly because of a motivation to evaluate whether infants and young children have "true number concepts"—that is, whether they attend to discrete number and enumerate sets as adults do. Some have concluded not only that infants and children attend to discrete number but that number itself must be a privileged domain because these concepts appear so early. However, even though experimenters have used sets of discrete items, children may not perceive or represent quantity in a discrete way. After examining this research, we found no reason to conclude that infants possess notions of exact number. In fact, there is reason to suspect that infants do not quantify number of discrete entities at all but rather represent amount of substance.

This suggests a different starting point for the development of quantitative concepts than the domain-specific accounts that have been so influential (e.g., Gelman, 1991; Wynn, 1997). Instead, infants may start out with an undifferentiated notion of quantity based on amount of stuff for both discrete and continuous entities, only later evolving different principles for handling these two types of quantity separately. If this account is correct, there should be evidence of an early sensitivity to continuous amount. In this chapter, we review the few studies that have examined this sensitivity. Even this limited literature supports the idea that infants and young children process continuous amount. Furthermore, there are indications that this ability developmentally precedes understanding of discrete number.

As in previous chapters, we focus on three quantitative abilities: (1) discrimination of amounts, (2) recognition of equivalence and ordinality, and (3) calculation. Also, as before, the studies we include all address children's concepts prior to mastery of conventional symbol systems. The studies reviewed here used absolute amounts of continuous substance and not relative quantities, such as fractions and proportions. In the case of discrete quantity, this would be analogous to focusing on the ability to compare two and three rather than the ability to compare $1/6$ and $3/4$ of a dozen. In the latter case, the quantities, though still discrete, are related to a whole unit (i.e., one dozen). Although relative quantities and absolute amounts are conceptually distinct, it is not always obvious from children's behavior or the requirements of a particular task which kind of quantity was used. In fact, as we will argue later on, nearly all quantitative tasks could be construed in terms of relative quantity. However, because the development of relative quantity concepts has unique complexities, we will discuss it separately in chapter 6. For now, we focus on studies in which participants could have used absolute amount of substance to reach a solution.

Discriminating between Amounts

Perhaps the most basic quantitative ability is detecting the difference between one amount and another. The ability to make such discriminations for discrete sets is one of the most robust and replicable in the infant literature. However, as we discussed in chapter 2, infants react only when there is a change in overall amount. They do not respond to changes in number alone. Until now, we have discussed this finding as it pertains to claims of numerical representation in infants. However, it also demonstrates a more basic fact: infants are sensitive to changes in continuous amount.

Gao, Levine, and Huttenlocher (2000) found more direct evidence of this sensitivity using a standard habituation experiment with continuous amounts. They habituated 5-month-old infants to either a ¼ full container or a ¾ full container of red liquid. Since identical containers were used in all cases, amount of liquid varied only along the vertical dimension. After the infants were habituated to one of these amounts, they were shown an identical container with either the same amount as in the habituation trials or a different amount. Infants looked significantly longer when a different amount of liquid was presented in the dishabituation trials. Thus, infants must have represented amount, as indicated by the height of the liquid in the container, with some degree of accuracy.

Further evidence that infants discriminate between amounts comes from an experiment on distance encoding in 5-month-olds (Newcombe, Huttenlocher, & Learmonth, 1999). In this experiment, a narrow 3-foot long sandbox was placed at a horizontal orientation in front of the infant. Then an object was hidden and recovered at a particular distance from the edge of the sandbox. This hiding-recovery sequence was repeated four times. At the next trial, the object was hidden and then recovered at either the correct distance or 6 inches away from the location of hiding. Infants looked significantly longer when the object emerged at the incorrect distance. As in the Gao et al. study, amount varied along only one dimension; amount of liquid varied along the vertical dimension and location varied along the horizontal dimension. Hence, it is not surprising that infants succeed at both of these problems at the same age.

These studies show that infants are sensitive to changes in continuous amount. This fact alone challenges the idea that discrete number concepts are privileged. At the least, this research indicates that infants are sensitive to both kinds of quantity.

Recognizing Relations between Amounts

As we noted in chapter 2, discrimination studies can tell us whether infants notice that two amounts are different, but they do not show that infants understand *why* the amounts are different. Such evidence can come only from studies that focus on quantitative relations—recognizing equivalence or ordinality. Evidence that infants recognize these relations for discrete quantity is scanty, but it is nonexistent for continuous amount, not because negative evidence has been obtained but because this topic has not been examined previously.

In contrast, there is some evidence that young children can recognize these relations. As we mentioned in chapter 3, Brainerd (1973a) found that 73% of kindergarten children could order multiple continuous amounts: children arranged three clay balls according to their weight or arranged three sticks according to length. Further evidence comes from one of our unpublished studies (Mix, Huttenlocher, & Levine, in preparation). We presented children with a linear scale that had a sad Cookie Monster on one end and a happy Cookie Monster on the other. The child's task was to order two sets of "cookies." The sets contained either whole cookies or fractional portions of cookies (see figure 5.1). Children as young as 3 years old performed significantly above chance on both whole number and fractional ordering items. In fact, performance was the same whether the cookies depicted whole number or fractional amounts. We varied the number of pieces in the fractional problems to ensure that they were solved on the basis of amount. For example, one and a quarter could be presented as one whole cookie and a quarter of a cookie, five quarters of a cookie, or several combinations of different sized pieces that resulted in one and a quarter cookies when combined. Thus, the number of discrete pieces could vary without changing the overall amount. Regardless of whether one and a quarter had the same, more, or fewer pieces than one and three quarters, children correctly judged one amount to be larger than another (e.g., one and three quarters to be larger than one and one quarter).

Children could have solved these cookie ordering problems in two ways. One would involve standardizing the amounts relative to some unit, such as a whole cookie. For example, where there were five quarter cookies versus one and a half cookies, children might have mentally combined four of the five quarters to make a whole cookie and then compared the totals ($1\frac{1}{4}$ vs. $1\frac{1}{2}$). Or children might have mentally combined the pieces to derive a representation of the total amount without regard for a whole unit. In this case, they would be using absolute amount of continuous substance rather than quantity relative to a whole.

In light of previous research, it is interesting that children performed so well on the Cookie Monster task. Gelman (1991) described an unpublished study from her lab in which children also were asked to order fractional amounts of circles on a linear scale. However, rather than asking children to order two amounts relative to each other, Gelman tested whether they could place a single amount (e.g., $1\frac{1}{2}$ circles) on a scale that already included whole number landmarks. She found that children had great difficulty with this task well into elementary school. In fact, they tended to err by placing the fractional amount on top of the whole number landmark with the same number of pieces (e.g., $1\frac{1}{2}$ circles on top of 2 whole circles).

Gelman interpreted children's failure as an inability to conceive of quantities between whole numbers. However, even if children cannot

Comparison Types

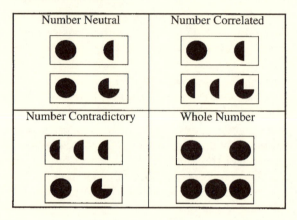

FIGURE 5.1 Sample stimuli from Mix et al.'s fraction ordering experiment.

comprehend such quantities (an issue we will address in chapter 6), they could solve her task by comparing the absolute amounts of "circle stuff"—the overall area included when the circle parts were combined. We know that children can do this from their performance on the Cookie Monster task. So why didn't it work for them in Gelman's experiment?

One important difference between the two tasks was that our version did not involve landmarks. As Piaget (1952) found, it is difficult for children to insert items into an existing series. This may be the reason why children did not place fractions in their correct positions in Gelman et al.'s task yet correctly ordered fractions relative to each other in our task.

Another possibility is that the whole number constraints Gelman (1991) observed were an artifact of her procedure. Although the number line she used had no numerals written on it, it may have looked enough like a standard number line to call the whole number landmarks to mind. Furthermore, Gelman and her colleagues reinforced a whole number interpretation of the task through a series of warm-up activities, such as asking children to say the conventional number that would come after each of the endpoints and having children practice by placing the two-circle landmark between the one- and three-circle landmarks. Because our Cookie Monster scale did not resemble a conventional number line and our procedure did not predispose children to view it as such, they may have been freer to see the problems in terms of continuous amounts or relative quantity.

The studies we reviewed indicate that children can recognize relations between continuous amounts of substance. Admittedly, much more developmental work has been completed using discrete number than using continuous amount. Still, the extant studies are sufficient to rule out the notion that continuous amount cannot be represented preverbally.

Calculation

In chapter 2, we reviewed evidence that infants understand quantitative transformations. Specifically, Wynn and others (Simon et al., 1995; Uller et al., 1999; Wynn, 1992) have shown that when infants see a small number of objects placed sequentially behind a screen, they are surprised when the screen is lowered to reveal a different number of objects. Because experimenters in these studies used displays of individual items, rather than lumps of continuous substance, many have concluded that infants can calculate over discrete number. However, it is also possible that infants mentally combine the amount of stuff in the separate items and respond to the solution that differs in amount. Because the published findings have been limited to small sets (e.g., two vs. one), the proportional difference in continuous amount is maximized. Therefore, even a rough estimate of continuous amount would suffice.

Aware of this potential confound in the calculation procedure, Wynn (1993) attempted to rule out the use of continuous amount with the following control. She presented a glass that was partially filled with liquid. This glass was then hidden behind a screen, and an additional amount of liquid was added to it. This permitted infants to see the action of pouring but not the resulting amount. At test, the screen was then dropped to reveal a glass with either the original amount of liquid or the correct amount following the transformation. Nine-month-olds looked equally long at these two outcomes. Wynn argued from these findings that "infants cannot represent continuous amounts of substance" because they did not react to changes in amount.

However, subsequent research has challenged this conclusion. Using Wynn's (1993) procedure, Gao et al. (2000) found that 9-month-olds did look significantly longer toward the starting amount (the incorrect solution) than they looked toward the transformed amount (the correct solution). Thus, babies are indeed sensitive to transformations in the amount of continuous quantity. One reason for the discrepancy between these results and Wynn's is that Wynn used two containers that differed in size and shape (i.e., a glass and a pitcher). Because Gao et al. used two identical containers, it may have been easier for infants to approximate the change in amount.

Furthermore, recall that Feigenson and Spelke (1998) tested infants using Wynn's procedure but varied the sizes of the dolls. For example, infants might see two small dolls placed sequentially behind a screen and then see a solution of two large dolls (correct number, incorrect mass) or one large doll (incorrect number, correct mass). Under these conditions, infants looked significantly longer toward the incorrect amount but not the incorrect number of dolls. So not only do infants appear to understand transformations in continuous amount, but this, rather than notions of discrete number, might actually form the basis of their response in Wynn's calculation paradigm.

Might preschool children also be able to solve calculation problems involving continuous amount? Recall Huttenlocher et al.'s (1994) finding that preschool children could produce the solutions to calculation problems involving discrete sets. For example, when children saw two objects that were then hidden beneath a cover and next saw a third object added to the hidden set, they were able to produce the resulting set of three objects without ever seeing the experimenter's total. Gao, Huttenlocher, and Levine (in preparation) tested the same ability in 4- to 6-year-olds using both discrete and continuous amounts. For now, we will focus on the results involving continuous quantity. In the continuous condition, an amount of red liquid was placed in a long vertical cylinder. Then a screen was raised and an amount of liquid was added to the hidden amount by pouring it from an identical container. The child's task was to indicate which of four choices showed the amount after the transformation. The correct answer and distractors differed by at least ⅛ of the total size of the container to ensure that children could choose correctly without using a unit measure. Gao et al. found that children as young as age 4 solved these calculation of amount problems. It is possible that younger children could also solve them if they were tested.

The research reviewed above demonstrates that infants and children respond to calculation problems using continuous amount in the same way they respond to parallel problems using discrete sets. There is no indication that children perform better on discrete calculation tasks. Furthermore, infants fail to respond to transformations in discrete number when overall amount is controlled (Feigenson & Spelke, 1998).

Thus, these experiments provide no reason to conclude that discrete number concepts are developmentally privileged.

One Representation?

The studies just reviewed show that infants and young children can perform quantitative tasks involving amounts of continuous substance. As we discussed in chapter 2, there is reason to think that infants use overall amount to perform discrete tasks as well. Perhaps infants and very young children do not estimate number in discrete sets of objects at all but instead estimate continuous amount. In other words, there may be only one representation at first that encompasses both kinds of quantity.

Discrete quantities could be represented as continuous amounts through at least two mechanisms. First, the amount of substance could be accumulated across the gaps between items—either by mentally shoving the items together or by measuring item by item while ignoring the gaps. Alternatively, quantity could be estimated based on the size of the overall region encompassed by the entire set of discrete entities, as if there were an envelope around the set, without any attention to the size of the individual objects or their proximity.

The extant studies seem to have ruled out this envelope hypothesis. Several studies have shown that infants still respond to a change in amount even when the lengths and arrangements of the sets are controlled (Antell & Keating, 1981; Clearfield & Mix, 1999; Starkey & Cooper, 1980; Starkey et al., 1990). This suggests that quantity is estimated instead by accumulating over the individuals.

If infants and young children do not represent sets of discrete objects in terms of number, but, rather, in terms of overall amount of substance, then perhaps they are using a single principle of quantification, regardless of the nature of the stimuli presented. To an adult, this seems quite odd. Could infants possibly combine an elephant and a car, obtaining a notion of overall amount of the two together? This would be sensible if infants failed to distinguish between types of entities when they are quantifying amount and focus instead on overall amount of substance. That would be to say that infants ignore the perceptual characteristics of objects when assessing quantity but rather treat them only as an amount of substance. There is reason to think that this is the case. Several studies have shown that infants focus on location or movement rather than features such as color or shape in tasks that involve individuation (Newcombe et al., 1999; Simon et al., 1995; Xu & Carey, 1996). For example, Newcombe et al. (1998) found that infants were surprised when an object reappeared at a different location from the one where it was originally hidden but not when a different object appeared in the same location as in the original hiding place.

Differentiation of Discrete and Continuous Quantity

At some point, children begin to quantify discrete sets of objects and continuous substances differently, both in encoding and transforming amount. This differentiation is inevitable because there are conceptual and functional differences between the two types of quantity. First, notions of discrete and continuous quantity are typically applied in different contexts. Quantification based on number is generally used for entities that change their character when subdivided (e.g., half of an elephant is no longer an elephant). In contrast, quantification based on amount is generally used for homogeneous substances that do not change their character when subdivided (e.g., sand, water). Of course, one can quantify some sets either way, depending on the goal of the quantifier. For example, cookies are usually counted, but they are sometimes quantified in terms of continuous substance, as when they are sold by the pound.

Second, the requirements for applying unit measures are different for discrete and continuous quantity. In both cases, applying unit measures involves subdividing the set and then tagging each portion with one unit. However, when unit measures are applied to discrete sets, the subdivision process is already done: discrete items are bounded and separate by definition. Of course, one must still keep track of which items have already been tagged, but this is not the same as the subdivision problem for continuous amounts. For continuous amounts, the person doing the quantifying must physically measure and separate the units himself. Thus, learning to apply unit measures to continuous amounts requires more knowledge and effort on the part of the measurer (Miller, 1984).

A final difference between continuous and discrete quantification is the level of precision possible. Number can be determined exactly by mapping the items in a set onto an ordered set of tags, such as the count words. This does not mean that discrete quantification is *always* exact. One could approximate the number of items in a set—for example, knowing that there are about 10 candies left in the box. However, it is at least possible to quantify discrete sets exactly. In contrast, quantification of continuous amount is always approximate. One can become relatively precise by using measuring devices and counting the number of measured units (e.g., the number of teaspoonfuls of sugar in a bowl). However, even if a unit measure is used, amount can be determined only to a certain level of accuracy because substance is infinitely divisible; it is always possible to become more accurate by using smaller units. For example, a seamstress could measure a length of cloth in meters, but there are still centimeters and millimeters and so on. Of course, when a unit measure is not applied, only rough estimates of quantity may be possible. Accuracy in this case may depend on the shape of the substance. For example, an irregularly shaped quantity of clay may be more difficult to estimate than a neat bar.

Let us now return to the critical developmental question: what leads children to see discrete and continuous quantities as distinct? How do they discover for themselves that these are different notions applied in different contexts? Given the preceding analysis, we propose that the emergence of exact measurement processes is one possible catalyst. These processes would include nonverbal representations of discrete number as well as conventional measurement tools. Huttenlocher et al. (1994) proposed that children acquire a symbolic one-to-one representation of number in early childhood (i.e., a mental model). This notion is supported by evidence that children represent discrete sets prior to learning conventional skills but only after a period of approximate responding (Huttenlocher et al., 1994; Mix, in preparation). However, such a one-to-one mapping could apply only to discrete sets (Huttenlocher et al., 1994). If children acquire a process that applies to one type of quantity but not the other, this could signal to them that continuous and discrete quantification are distinct.

This process of differentiation would continue as children acquire measurement conventions. Measuring discrete quantities is easier than measuring continuous amount. Because discrete sets are already subdivided, one need only count the units. However, as we noted, continuous amounts must be divided into equal units before they are enumerated. Because of these differences, children learn to measure discrete quantities before they learn to measure continuous amounts (Miller, 1984). Once children discover that applying conventional unit measures leads to greater accuracy, they may be especially motivated to use them whenever they can. This could lead to further exploration of the situations in which discrete measurement processes can be applied. As children discover when these work and when they don't, they would also discover the difference between discrete and continuous quantification.

In fact, there is empirical evidence that supports this account. First, it is clear that children measure discrete sets before they can measure continuous amount. Several studies have shown that preschoolers can measure discrete sets via one for you, one for me distribution (Frydman & Bryant, 1988; Miller, 1984). For example, Miller asked preschoolers to divide pretend foods between two turtles. Starting at age 3, children successfully divided sets of candies using distributive counting. However, there is no evidence that children of this age can use measurement to quantify continuous substance. In Miller's study, children failed to use equal units to divide continuous substances (such as lengths of clay "spaghetti") until school age. Similarly, Piaget reported that children were unable to use continuous unit measures in a building task. He asked children to build a block tower to match another tower in height.

Children were given sticks of various lengths that could be used to measure height. The task was designed to prevent children from using nonmeasurement strategies, such as counting the number of blocks. Under these conditions, children younger than 7 years simply could not determine whether the heights of the towers matched—they did not understand how to use the sticks as measuring units to figure out the answer.

Preschoolers have difficulty thinking about unit measures with continuous quantity even when they do not have to apply the measure themselves. Huntley-Fenner (1999) had 3- to 5-year-olds watch while objects were placed into containers or cupfuls of sand were poured into containers. When asked which of two containers had more, children chose on the basis of number for the objects but did not choose on the basis of number of cupfuls for the sand. Rather, they based their judgments on rate and chose the container that had sand poured into it more quickly. Thus, children count units of continuous substance later than they count discrete objects. Differences in exposure may partially account for this finding. Children often see others explicitly counting discrete objects but less often witness others measuring continuous amounts. Even when they do see measuring, they probably rarely see unit measures being accumulated explicitly. In measuring length, for example, one would likely use a yardstick to determine that a length is 32 inches, rather than successively applying a 1- inch measure 32 times.

These studies indicate that children use conventional units to precisely quantify discrete entities well before they use unit measures to quantify continuous amounts. If we are correct that this difference in timing helps children to differentiate discrete from continuous quantity conceptually, then we may predict that once children gain the accuracy that comes with applying unit measures, they should prefer discrete quantification over continuous quantification. However, this preference should be limited to small sets at first because children learn to apply unit measures to these sets first. During this period, children should continue to quantify continuous amounts and large discrete sets using their preexisting representation of amount. Hence, differences in the way discrete and continuous amounts are quantified should first emerge for small numerosities, whereas larger numerosities will be quantified as they had been earlier, like continuous amounts.

Evidence of this basic pattern appeared in Gao et al.'s (in preparation) study of nonverbal calculation in 4- to 6-year-olds. Recall that children saw an amount of red liquid placed in a cylinder; then a screen was raised and more liquid was added to the hidden amount. The children's task was to indicate which of four quantities matched the resulting amount or solution. In addition to testing this continuous version, Gao et al. also tested calculation of discrete quantities using the same cylindrical apparatus. In the discrete condition, red blocks were used instead of liquid. A number of blocks were placed in the cylinder, a screen was raised, and then more blocks were added. To parallel the pouring of the liquid in the continuous condition, these blocks were dropped into the cylinder from an identical cylinder. This procedure allowed a direct comparison of performance across continuous and discrete quantities in the same task.

When performance on the two conditions was compared, 6-year-olds were more accurate in the discrete condition (see table 5.1). However, this was true only for small numerosity problems (i.e., solutions of 3, 4, or 5). At higher numerosities (i.e., 6 and 7), there was no difference between performance in the discrete and continuous conditions. Apparently 6-year-olds performed better on the low numerosity discrete problems because they had discovered a way to represent these quantities more accurately than either continuous amounts or large discrete sets. For example, they might have used conventional counting to keep track of the small numbers of blocks. Thus, the pattern here is consistent with the hypothetical pattern we proposed.

Studies of sharing also indicate that after children learn to keep track of small numbers accurately using unit measures, they tend to favor number over amount of substance for quantification. When Piaget (Piaget et al., 1960) had young children indicate how a "cookie" could be divided fairly among particular numbers of individuals, he found that preschoolers divided the cookie in terms of the number of pieces rather than amount of substance. Based on the preschoolers' divisions, individuals recieved very different amounts of cookie. Miller's (1984) sharing study also showed that preschool children tried to achieve equality of number of pieces but did not focus on equality of amount (i.e., the sizes of the pieces). A striking example is the behavior of a subset of the preschool children who, when they came up one piece short, resolved the situation by breaking one recipient's piece in two. Although this achieved equality of number, it clearly did not achieve equality of amount.

TABLE 5.1. Average Scores (S.D.) by Age, Numerosity, and Task

Age	Small Numerosity		Large Numerosity	
	Continuous task	Discrete task	Continuous task	Discrete task
4	0.75 (1.76)	1.41 (1.04)	1.08 (0.89)	0.75 (0.55)
5	2.21 (1.57)	2.41 (1.89)	1.54 (1.16)	1.00 (0.72)
6	1.75 (1.45)	3.38 (1.99)	1.78 (1.29)	2.23 (1.63)

Note: Full score = 4.

Conclusions

When the evidence related to continuous and discrete quantity is considered all together, it forms a coherent story about the development of quantification early in life. This development starts with only one principle of quantification in infancy based on amount of substance, which applies to both continuous quantity and sets of discrete objects. The single principle for quantification might begin to differentiate around 2½ years of age when children develop an exact representation of discrete number; however, additional testing with older infants and toddlers may reveal that it begins even earlier. This differentiation would continue as children learn to quantify using conventional unit measures because of differences in task demands for the two kinds of measurement. At the early stages of this conceptual split, children may focus on small sets because they can represent these nonverbally. At this point, large sets of discrete objects may be quantified in the same way as continuous quantities, through estimates of overall amount. However, as children gain proficiency with conventional skills, such as counting, they should extend their concept of discrete quantity to sets of any size.

Of course, the scenario we propose here is not the only possible account of the existing data. However, we believe it currently provides the best fit. Much remains to be learned about quantitative development during this period, especially relating to continuous amount. As more investigations are completed, we hope to determine whether our explanation accurately captures the interplay of these quantitative concepts.

6

Relative Quantity

In this chapter we turn to another important notion of quantity: relative quantity. Although quantification is often thought of as providing an absolute measure of quantity, the judgment of quantity is always relative to some type of measure. Discrete number is determined by a one-to-one mapping between a set of objects and an ordered set of tags. In our counting system this ordered set consists of the natural numbers. Continuous quantity is determined via an imposed measurement unit to obtain an accurate measure of amount. Our conventional system includes measures such as inches or feet for size or distance, minutes or seconds for time, and so forth. However, relative quantity usually refers to another sort of notion conventionalized in terms of fractions or ratios. For example, a quantity judgment is said to be relative when it is coded as half a box of candies rather than as six candies or half a glass of milk rather than as four ounces of milk.

Even at school age, children have difficulty acquiring the conventional forms used to represent relative quantity. However, even though a child cannot solve the symbolic problem $1/2 + 1/4$, he still may know that half a cookie added to one quarter of a cookie equals three-quarters of a cookie. In other words, concepts of relative quantity may emerge before children learn the relevant conventions. This issue has taken on important theoretical implications in recent years. One account of quantitative development posits the ability to represent and reason about discrete number as an innate endowment (e.g., Gelman, 1991; Wynn, 1995, 1997). In this view, nature has selected number as a domain for which humans are born with special abilities. The proponents of this account argue that because the innate mechanism cannot represent amounts between whole numbers (i.e., fractions and proportions), relative quantity concepts should emerge late and with great difficulty (Gelman, 1991; Wynn, 1995).

Indeed, children acquire the conventions for relative quantities late and with difficulty. For example, Gelman (1991) reported that children tend to make "whole number errors" on tasks involving fractions. In one task, children were asked which of two fractions was the larger amount (e.g., $1/4$ vs. $1/2$). They tended to reverse the order of these fractions, as if they thought about them in terms of whole numbers. That is, they responded that $1/4$ was larger than $1/2$, apparently because four is larger than two. But such evidence does not separate knowledge about conventional symbols from knowledge about the underlying concepts. Even if children understand relative quantities, they may be confused by the use of numerals to stand for whole quantities and fractional quantities in which the meaning of the same numeral can be very different (e.g., 4 vs. $1/4$).

As the following review will show, children do understand relative quantity before they learn conventional symbols. In fact, the lag between demonstration of this understanding and mastery of the conventional symbols suggests that this latter step, rather than a limit to their quantitative representations, is the stumbling block for most children. Nonetheless, not all relative quantity concepts are easy to acquire. While some relative quantity concepts emerge quite early, others emerge rather late. In this chapter, we will specify the factors that contribute to the difficulty of relative quantity problems.

We begin by reviewing the evidence of relative quantity concepts that has been gathered using nonconventional measures to complete the background on nonverbal quantitative development we provided in previous chapters. The acquisition of conventional fraction skills will be discussed in chapter 8. As before, we present our initial review in terms of the skills being tested: recognition of equivalence and ordinality relations and understanding transformations.

This review covers only studies with preschool children because, to our knowledge, no studies have tested infants' perception of relative quantity. However, we should note that infants may well be using relative quantity in the experiments thus far. Consider the standard habituation procedure—infants are habituated to several equivalent sets and then are tested with novel displays of the same number and a different number. We argued in chapter 5 that infants might be attending to the absolute amount of area or contour length in these displays rather than discrete number. It is also possible that they are attending to the amount represented in the displays relative to some other aspect of the display, such as the background. Because the habituation displays are always presented in an area of fixed size (e.g., a series of identical cards or slides, a computer screen, etc.), when the quantity of items changes, the proportion of foreground to background also changes. Infants may be responding to this change rather than to the change in absolute amount that researchers have intended to test.

In fact, notions of relative quantity may be more primitive than those for absolute quantity whether discrete or continuous. According to the Gestalt psychologists, the human perceptual system is constructed so that judgments of stimulus magnitude are inherently relative. Evidence for this view comes from studies showing that judgments of stimulus magnitude, such as of object size, line length, weight, and so forth, are affected by their context. For example, the perceived size of a square is affected by whether it occurs in the context of larger or smaller squares. Inspired by these ideas, Bryant (1974) completed a series of studies to determine whether relative judgment is the basic way children determine stimulus magnitude. He compared young children's ability to respond either relatively or absolutely to stimulus size. One group of 4-year-olds was trained to respond either to the larger or the smaller of two squares, regardless of its absolute size. Another group was trained to respond to a square of a particular absolute size, regardless of its size relative to another square. Bryant found that the children learned to make the relative judgment more easily than the absolute judgment.

If the Gestaltist view of quantity judgment is correct, then one might expect a primitive notion of relative quantity to emerge early in development. As the following review shows, such a notion is clearly evident by early childhood. Although there is no direct evidence of this ability in infants, we know from the studies reviewed in chapter 5 that infants can discriminate between continuous amounts. As we discussed, the use of a unit measure is important in establishing the amount of a continuous substance accurately, and this ability emerges around age 5. Hence, the ability of infants or very young children to discriminate amount of continuous substance must be based on some mechanism other than application of a unit measure. Comparing one part of a display to another might provide the needed mechanism.

We turn now to the kind of quantity judgments that people usually associate with relative quantity. In contrast to comparisons in which one directly compares two perceptually present amounts, this type of judgment is based on comparisons where there is a distinction between a target quantity and a reference quantity. Proportion is critical, not the absolute amount of the target quantity or the reference quantity alone. We begin by considering children's recognition of ordinality and equivalence among such quantities.

Recognizing Relations between Relative Quantities

In this chapter, we focus on tasks in which the comparison of proportions cannot be achieved by using a comparison of absolute quantity. For example, you could determine that half an orange is equal to half an orange by comparing the absolute amount of orange in both pieces. Comparing the amount would be straightforward because the two pieces would be nearly identical. However, determining that half an orange is equal in proportion to half a watermelon requires an awareness of relative quantity. In this case, the pieces differ along many dimensions and the absolute amounts are misleading.

Several studies have shown that young children can recognize equivalence between proportions. Goswami (1989) found that by age 4, children could pick out equivalent proportions for objects of different shapes in an analogical reasoning task. For example, if children were shown that $\frac{1}{2}$ of a circle went with $\frac{1}{2}$ of a rectangle, they could judge that $\frac{1}{4}$ of a circle went with $\frac{1}{4}$ of a rectangle.

Using a matching task, Spinillo and Bryant (1991) found evidence of a similar ability. They showed 4- to 7-year-olds a picture of a small rectangle divided into blue and white portions. Then, they asked the child to decide which of two larger block models, oriented differently from the smaller rectangular picture, had the same proportion of blue and white as a smaller rectangular picture. Even the youngest children could make judgments of proportion in this task.

Sophian and Crosby (1999) also found that preschool children could match geometric figures on the basis of spatial proportion. For example, they showed children a rectangle that had a particular ratio between length and width. The children then indicated which of two other rectangles had the same ratio. An identity match was not possible because both choices were a different size than the standard. Four-year-olds, the youngest children tested, performed significantly above chance even when the ratio difference between the two choice rectangles was small.

Finally, evidence suggests that children can recognize proportional equivalence in a map reading task. Map reading involves relative quantity because the size of the whole space in the real world is larger than that in the map and the target is located proportionally to this size difference. Huttenlocher, Newcombe, and Vasilyeva (1999) gave $3\frac{1}{2}$- to 4-year-olds the simplest of maps—a dot placed in a one-dimensional space—that could be used to find a hidden object in a much larger one-dimensional sandbox. All of the 4-year-olds and about 50% of the $3\frac{1}{2}$-year-olds succeeded on this task. The children could determine locations involving any proportion of the distance across the rectangle. Thus, under some conditions, the ability to recognize proportional equivalence appears quite early.

Other studies have examined whether children can recognize ordinal relations among proportions. A direct test would be to have children line up a set of proportions from smallest to largest, but few studies have taken this approach. For those that have, it is unclear whether children responded based on relative amount or absolute amount. For example, recall that Gelman's (1991) fraction ordering task involved placing different quantities of a circle (e.g., one and one-half circles) where they belonged on a number line with circle landmarks (i.e., one, two, and three circles). Although the test amounts were relative quantities, children might not have viewed the task as such. Because all the circles were the same size, it would be possible to solve this task by comparing the absolute amount of circle stuff on the test cards with the absolute amounts of circle stuff on the landmarks.

To provide clear evidence that children can order relative quantities, tasks are needed that cannot be solved via absolute amount. The literature on children's understanding of probability has used such tasks, beginning with the classic work of Piaget and Inhelder (1975). They presented children with quantity per unit problems that involved desired objects per total set of objects. The child's task was to determine which set had a higher proportion of a target item. For example, the child was shown two jars, each of which contained a mixture of objects, such as red and white counters. The proportions of the objects were different in each of the jars. For example, one jar might have four red and eight white counters while the other jar had three red and three white counters. The child was asked to choose which container they should draw from in order to get, for example, a red counter. Piaget found that rather than choosing the container with the greater relative number of target objects, children chose the container with the greater absolute number of target objects. So children would say that the jar with four out of twelve red counters is more likely to yield a red counter than the jar with three out of six red counters. This error usually persists until 10 years of age.

Clearly, Piaget's task was quite difficult—taking years longer for children to understand than the equivalence tasks described above. One reason might be that the Piagetian task requires not only an ordinal judgment but also an understanding of the probabilistic implications of that judgment. In other words, children have to know that the greater proportion also yields the higher probability of obtaining a desired outcome on a random draw. However, subsequent studies have revealed a sense of ordinality for relative quantities in much younger children, even when probability judgments are involved. Singer and Lovett (1991) told children a story about a bug who is happy to land on flowers but unhappy to land on a spider that might eat him. The child's task was to judge how happy the bug would be with each of a series of sets consisting of a mixture of flowers and spiders. The children expressed their judgments by moving a cursor on a continuous rating scale. For example, given a set with three spiders and seven flowers, children might rate the bug's happiness relatively high. Indeed, children in these studies consistently indicated that the bug would be happier when the set had a higher proportion of flowers. This is not exactly the same as making an explicit ordinality judgment because children were never asked to compare two sets directly. However, over the course of the experiment, their ratings resulted in an ordering of the sets.

Sophian, Garyantes, and Chang (1997) also found evidence that children could order relative quantities earlier than Piaget had claimed. They used a task similar to Piaget's in that it involved choosing which of two relative quantities would lead to a desired outcome. The goal was to feed some hungry pizza monsters. In one condition, the target quantity varied while the reference quantity was constant. For example, the choice was between half a cup and one whole cup of "pizzas" (orange lentils) to be shared among three pizza monsters. Even 5-year-olds performed perfectly on this task. In a second condition, the reference quantity varied and the target quantity was constant. In this case, the choice was whether the pizza monster should share his half a cup of pizzas with two or four friends. Not until age 7 could children succeed on this version of the task. However, in both cases children could make an ordinal judgment on proportion years earlier than they typically succeed in Piaget's task.

Jeong, Levine, and Huttenlocher (in preparation; see Levine, Jeong, & Gao, 1999) also carried out a proportional reasoning study much like Piaget's in that children were asked to make judgments about the likelihood of a particular draw. However, in this task one of the conditions involved continuous rather than discrete quantities. Six-, 8- and 10-year-old children were shown donut-shaped forms of different sizes. Each of these forms had red and blue regions (see figure 6.1). The division into red and blue regions was made in three different ways: (1) the regions were continuous and undifferentiated, (2) each colored region was subdivided into countable subregions but the subparts of each region were adjacent to each other, and (3) the red and blue subparts were intermixed around the donut-shaped form.

Children were shown a pointer that could stop on either a red or blue region and were told that if it landed on red they would get a sticker. On the test trials children were shown two different sized donuts that varied in the proportion of red and blue. Children were asked to choose which donut they would prefer to spin the pointer on. Clearly the correct choice was the donut with the larger proportion of red. When the regions were continuous rather than subdivided into units, children as young as 6 years had some success. However, they were totally unable to deal with the discrete condition in which the colored subparts were intermixed. This condition is most similar to

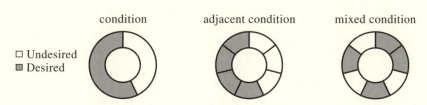

FIGURE 6.1 Children's performance on Gao et al.'s continuous reasoning task.

Piaget's in which two types of items were intermixed in each of two jars. In fact, children do not begin to succeed on this condition until about age 10, the same age as children begin to succeed on Piaget's task. Children apparently relied on the relative quantity of red and blue which was easiest to discern in the continuous condition.

After we have reviewed the literature on calculation with relative quantities, we will outline the sources of difficulty that determine whether a particular relative quantity task will emerge sooner or later developmentally. For now, the literature we have reviewed clearly indicates that children are capable of recognizing relations among proportions. This ability is impressive because it involves relating relations—a level of abstraction higher than that required for relating absolute amounts. Still, the early emergence of these concepts is not surprising if relative quantity is as conceptually basic as the Gestaltists and others have argued. Admittedly, the age ranges for these studies are somewhat higher than for the absolute quantity tasks already reviewed. However, younger children have not been tested on the most basic proportion tasks, such as choosing a matching proportion between two choices (e.g., ¼ of a circle = ¼ square vs. ½ square). Future research using such tasks might reveal an understanding of relative quantities in even younger children.

Calculation

We know from previous chapters that infants and children carry out quantitative transformations years before they master conventional arithmetic. This has been shown in several studies that used a nonverbal calculation procedure. A quantity is shown and then hidden, an amount is added to or subtracted from the hidden quantity, and the child indicates he knows the resulting amount by either producing it, pointing to it, or looking longer toward an incorrect solution. Previous studies have focused on absolute amounts; however, we recently used this approach to test whether children can solve such problems involving relative quantities (Mix, Levine, & Huttenlocher, 1999).

In this study, children were given two sets of calculation problems: one involving fractions and another involving whole numbers. In the fraction problems, children first saw a portion of a circle placed in a circle-shaped hole (e.g., $\frac{1}{2}$). This portion was then hidden behind a screen. Then a portion of the circle was either added to or subtracted from the hidden portion (e.g., $\frac{1}{4}$ was taken away). Children saw the piece being added or subtracted but could not see the resultant amount. They then chose the solution from a set of four pictures that showed different portions of a whole circle. The whole number problems were the same except that sets of black dots were used as stimuli (see chapter 3 for a detailed description of this procedure). We found that 4- and 5-year-olds could solve the fraction problems. When we tested 3-year-olds, they performed at chance levels, even though all three age groups solved parallel whole number problems.

In a second experiment, we tested whether children could solve more complex problems involving mixed numbers. We presented the problems as described but used up to three whole circles (e.g., problems such as $2\frac{1}{2} - 1\frac{3}{4}$ or $1\frac{1}{2} + \frac{1}{2}$). In this experiment, 6- and 7-year-olds performed significantly above chance, but 4- and 5-year-olds did not. Although this age is later than that when children solve similar problems involving absolute amount or smaller fractions, it is still much younger than when children learn the conventional algorithms for mixed number problems in school. In fact, a teacher questionnaire confirmed that none of the children in this study had been taught even the verbal labels for fractions. Thus children can reach calculation solutions that fall between whole units based on a nonverbal representation, an unexpected finding given claims that the preverbal representation of quantity cannot handle fractions (Gelman, 1991; Wynn, 1995, 1997).

What Children Know about Relative Quantity

The question of whether children can understand relative quantity is theoretically significant. As we have said, some views hold that quantitative development is rooted in an innate representation of discrete number (Gelman, 1991; Wynn, 1995, 1997). These views predict that notions of relative quantity should emerge late and with difficulty because the nonverbal system cannot represent amounts between whole units. In contrast, we have pursued the possibility that number concepts grow out of an undifferentiated sense of continuous and discrete quantity. Further, we have proposed that the mechanism by which infants estimate amount is based on relative quantity and in fact have argued that virtually all studies of quantitative development have used tasks that could be solved by relating one part to another. In this view, not only should children be capable of understanding relative quantity but this understanding might actually form the foundation of early quantitative development.

Our review of the studies related to this issue lends support to this proposal. Clearly, children can understand relative quantity. This understanding appears as early as 3 1/2 years of age, the youngest age tested thus far. Perhaps future studies will reveal the same ability in even younger children. Our review also shows that children succeed on a variety of relative quantity tasks much earlier than they are typically taught the conventional symbols and procedures for fractions and proportions. So they must be using a nonverbal process instead. These two facts alone challenge the view that early quantitative concepts are limited to whole, discrete number.

However, if relative quantity is the conceptual primitive upon which subsequent development builds, shouldn't children perform exceptionally well on all relative quantity tasks? Instead, the extant evidence shows that children readily perform some tasks in preschool but struggle with others well into fifth grade. In fact, there is often a wide age range of competence within the same experimental paradigm. Why? This variability across tasks does not necessarily indicate that relative quantity concepts as a whole emerge late. Even if some sense of relative quantity is conceptually primitive, it does not mean that it emerges full-blown. Relative quantity concepts likely grow over childhood, and this growth may underlie children's variable performance across different relative quantity tasks. In the remainder of this chapter, we analyze how these tasks differ and what performance on these different tasks implies about quantitative development.

Why Are Some Relative Quantity Tasks More Difficult than Others?

The relative quantity tasks we reviewed differ along several dimensions. In this section, we identify four key dimensions that can explain why children succeed on some tasks earlier than others. These dimensions include (1) whether the relation between quantities is implied or explicit, equivalence or ordinality, (2) whether the quantities are discrete or continuous, (3) whether the target or reference quantities are manipulated, and (4) whether the quantities are related to one whole, several wholes, or a measurement unit. This analysis not only accounts for the relative difficulty of these tasks but also reveals specific developmental changes in relative quantity concepts that occur in early childhood.

The Relation Being Tested: Equality, Ordinality, and No Explicit Comparison

One source of variation in difficulty for relative quantity tasks concerns the relation being tested. First, judgments of equality of two proportions seem to be easier than judgments of ordinality. We reviewed several studies showing that 4-year-olds can recognize equivalence between various proportional amounts (Goswami, 1989; Huttenlocher, Newcombe, & Vasilyeva, in preperation; Sophian & Crosby, 1999; Spinillo & Bryant, 1991). In contrast, problems involving ordinal judgments between proportions emerged somewhat later. For example, Jeong et al. (in preparation) found that 6-year-olds were just beginning to choose the donut that yielded the higher probability of landing on the target color.

A second trend is that tasks that do not require an explicit comparison across sets are also easier than tasks that do. For example, very young children demonstrate an implicit awareness of ordinality by rating one proportion at a time, as in Singer and Lovett's (1991) experiments with the bug landing in a flower patch. In tasks such as Piaget and Inhelder's (1975) probability judgments, children had to compare two relative quantities directly. Previous research on children's comparisons has shown that responding to a single instance is easier and emerges earlier than generating a response that requires comparing two or more entities (see Smith, 1993). Thus, relative quantity comparisons are much like comparisons in general. This is also similar to the trend we discussed in chapter 3 regarding children's recognition of numerical equivalence. Recall that the ability to judge two sets to be equivalent (and thus perform an explicit comparison between sets) emerges later than infants' habituation to different kinds of sets.

Continuous Quantity versus Discrete Sets of Elements

Another trend is that relative quantity tasks involving continuous amount are easier than those involving discrete number. As we noted, Jeong et al. (in preparation) found that 6-year-olds could judge ordinality of proportions as long as the amounts to be compared were presented as uninterrupted blocks of color. When the same task was used with discrete sections of color, either adjacent or intermixed, children failed until they were 8 or 10 years of age, respectively. Studies that have shown preschool children can judge equivalence of proportions have also used continuous amounts. In contrast, studies that have tested ordinal judgments of proportions (which emerge quite late) have all used mixtures of discrete entities. So the difference between children's performance on equivalence and ordinality tasks may be attributable, at least in part, to a difference between performance with discrete and continuous quantity.

In fact, this conclusion is supported by the results of several new studies that, like Jeong et al.'s, have looked specifically at the relative difficulty of discrete and continuous versions of the same task. Freeman and Goswami (1997) found that preschoolers performed better on relative quantity problems involving continuous quantities, such as pizzas, than they do on discrete quantities, such as number of candies. On the continuous task, an experimenter had a pizza divided into eight equally sized pieces, and the child had a pizza of the same size divided into four pieces. The experimenter took away a certain proportion of her pizza ($\frac{1}{4}$, $\frac{1}{2}$ or $\frac{3}{4}$), and the child's task was to take away the same proportion from her pizza. On the discrete task, the procedure was the same, but now the experimenter had a set of eight candies and the child had a set of four candies. Children performed much better on the continuous pizza task than on the parallel candy task, which suggests that thinking about proportions of discrete quantity is particularly difficult.

The earlier emergence of competence with continuous proportions is also reflected in children's acquisition of verbal labels for fractions. Hunting and Davis (1991) found that the same word, "half," is more easily applied to a single whole object than to a set. They noted that adults might use fraction terms to describe wholes more frequently than for sets, and this difference in input might lead to the difference in acquisition. However, it is also possible that this difference in acquisition reflects a cognitive bias on the part of the children. In fact, greater talk about relative quantity for continuous amounts no doubt reflects the greater frequency with which relative quantity is considered in this context. That is, because these notions of relative quantity are more often useful for continuous wholes, they may be more often described for continuous wholes and learned earlier in this context.

It makes sense that children would deal with relative quantity for continuous quantities earlier than for sets of discrete entities. They may get more direct input because continuous quantities often appear in containers. Containers maintain the form of certain substances, such as liquids. Thus, more likely a continuous substance rather than a discrete set would be quantified in terms of the portion of the container it occupies. This is to say that the judgment of relative quantity for continuous substance is one that is frequently encountered and hence may be acquired early. Because children cannot quantify continuous amount using unit measures until 5 to 6 years of age, they might instead use comparison between two perceptually present quantities for a considerable period of time. In contrast, children can quantify sets of discrete quantities in terms of one-to-one procedures quite early, certainly by age 4, and this may limit their need to quantify in terms of relative amount. Moreover, applying relative quantity to number situations requires knowing the number in the target subset as well as the number in either the remaining subset or the total. Thus, relative amount in this numeric sense may require mastery of conventional mathematical skills, whereas relative amount for continuous substances may be perceptually available.

However, in apparent contrast to these findings, several studies have found that children are better at sharing with discrete sets of objects than with continuous substances (e.g., Frydman & Bryant, 1988; Hunting & Sharpley, 1988; Miller, 1984). For example, Hunting and Sharpley found that 4- to 7-year-olds were better able to distribute discrete sets of objects than continuous amounts among several dolls. As noted in chapter 5, Miller found that when children were asked to partition a set of discrete objects and were one piece short, they simply broke one piece in half. Thus, they equated the number of pieces but not the amount given to each participant.

Although these studies may seem to show that understanding of the relative quantity per person emerges earlier for discrete than for continuous quantity, fair sharing of discrete objects may indicate only that children have learned the "one for me, one for you" rule, which would not require a real understanding that the quantity per person needs to be equal. Even if children had a deeper understanding of relative quantity per person, continuous quantities may be more difficult to partition because this partitioning involves the additional step of splitting the substance fairly. As we have said, without physically measuring the substance, one must rely on an estimate of amount. In contrast, discrete quantities are already subdivided. Thus, the same trend we identified for absolute quantity seems to hold for relative quantity. That is, continuous amount may initially be quantified more easily than discrete sets when only approximations are required. However, when children begin to use conventions to generate exact responses, this preference will shift to discrete quantities because these do not involve the added problem of equal subdivision. Furthermore, when children learn to count, they may overextend counting to continuous amounts.

When Target or Reference Quantities Are Held Constant

To really demonstrate an understanding of relative quantity, one should be able to perform tasks that involve a change in both the target (numerator) and the reference (denominator) quantities. For example, when $2/3$ is compared to $4/6$, the proportion is the same because the target and reference quantities have been multiplied by the same factor. Similarly, if a map of a space is 6 inches across, a location at its center is represented as 3 inches from the side of the map. If that map is applied to a real space that is 2 miles across, then the location that corresponds to the center on the map would be located 1 mile from the edge of the real space represented by the map. All of the studies reviewed thus far have used tasks like this.

However, one can construct proportional tasks with a fixed target or reference quantity. These cases are not really relative because when either quantity is held constant, one can judge amount by focusing on just the quantity that varies, not proportion. Still, because these cases arise when children learn about conventional fractions, it is worth considering what has been demonstrated preconventionally. Moreover, according to some evidence, performance on relative quantity problems is affected by differences in which quantity—target or reference—is held constant.

If the reference quantity is held constant, that quantity can be ignored in evaluating overall amount. For example, when comparing $^3/_5$ to $^2/_5$, one can focus on just the number of target parts while ignoring the reference quantity. Notice that as the target quantity increases, the overall amount increases. Thus, there is a direct relation between the target quantity and overall amount. Now consider what happens if the target quantity is held constant, as in $^4/_5$ versus $^4/_6$. In this case, the two reference quantities can be compared and the target quantities can be ignored. Note, however, that as the reference quantity increases, the overall amount decreases. Therefore, this case presents an inverse relation between the reference quantity and the overall amount.

Evidence shows that it is easier for children to deal with the direct relation between the target quantity and the overall amount than with the inverse relation between the reference quantity and the overall amount. Recall that Sophian, Garyantes, and Chang (1997) studied whether 5- to 7-year-olds understood problems in which either the target quantity or the reference quantity was held constant while the other varied. The children's task was to select between two amounts of food for a hungry Pizza Monster. Sophian et al. found that even 5-year-olds performed near ceiling on this task when the reference quantity was fixed. However, when the target quantity was fixed and there was an inverse relation between the reference quantity and overall amount, children performed poorly, until age 7.

The Relation to the Unit: Part-Part, Part-Whole, Multiple Wholes, and Measurement Units

Relative quantities are distinguished from estimates of absolute quantity by the fact that they involve a comparison or relation between amounts, which can take several forms. Some have argued that the type of comparison affects the difficulty of a relative quantity task (e.g., Spinillo & Bryant, 1991). One form of comparison uses a whole or total as the reference quantity. This whole or total forms an upper bound where a single whole is the universe under consideration; for example, objects of a particular kind per total objects (e.g., chocolate candies per set of all candies), desired outcomes per total outcomes (e.g., heads per coin tosses). Part-whole relations are usually embodied when we use conventional symbols for fractions. For example, one-half has meaning only in relation to some whole unit—half a dozen, half an apple, and so forth.

A second kind of relative quantity comparison involves dividing a whole or total into two parts. In such problems, relative quantity can be viewed in terms of the target part related to the remaining part (i.e., a part-part relation). Thus, half of an apple would be defined as one of two equal portions of a whole apple. In conventional terms, this would be the same as giving $\frac{1}{4}$ meaning only by comparing it to its complement, $\frac{3}{4}$. Thus, you could say that $\frac{1}{4}$ versus $\frac{3}{4}$ is a different proportion from $\frac{1}{2}$ versus $\frac{1}{2}$ because the relation between the parts is different. Some investigators have argued that the part-part relation is the easiest for children to comprehend and the first to emerge (Spinillo & Bryant, 1991).

A third form of relative quantity comparison is an extension of the part-whole relation that involves multiple wholes, represented conventionally as mixed numbers—fractional amounts that fall between whole units (e.g., $2\frac{1}{2}$). Even more than fractions that occur between zero and one, mixed numbers emphasize the relation to a whole unit. If the innate constraints view is correct and children cannot represent quantities between whole units, then this kind of relative quantity should be especially difficult. In fact, our research indicates that these comparisons are more difficult than a simple part-part or part-whole comparison. However, as we argue later, this difficulty does not seem to be rooted in an innate limitation.

Finally, a target quantity can be relativized to a measurement unit that is itself a relative quantity. This type of relativization can also be used to measure quantity accurately within a domain such as number of seconds per minute, number of feet per mile, and so forth. Distinct from this is the relativization of a target quantity in one domain to a reference quantity from another domain; for example, spatial extent per unit time, weight per unit volume, and so forth. Such cases do not involve a part-whole relation in any sense. As we will see, this kind of relativization emerges quite late.

Part-Part versus Part-Whole Relations First, consider how the differences between part-part and part-whole relations could contribute to problem difficulty. When a part is compared to a whole, the quantities are hierarchically related. In contrast, when a part is compared to another part, the relation is between two parts at the same level. Piaget's class-inclusion studies showed that young children have difficulty in conceptualizing hierarchical part-whole relations. In one experiment, children were shown a set of flowers that included tulips and daffodils. Then they were asked a part-whole question, such as whether there were more flowers or more tulips in the set. Children responded incorrectly to this type of question until they were about 6 years of age. They seemed to interpret the question as though they were being asked whether there were more daffodils or tulips because they responded based on the relative numbers of these two kinds of flowers. Either/or questions do not usually involve a comparison across two levels; rather, they more typically involve a comparison of two subsets at the same level, such as whether there are more tulips or more daffodils. Thus, children's difficulty on Piaget's task may be attributable to the form of the question rather than to difficulty with part-whole reasoning. However, it is also possible that a hierarchical relation of part to whole is conceptually difficult and would appear even on a nonverbal task.

The view that part-part relations are understood before part-whole relations gains some support from Spinillo and Bryant's (1991) study described earlier. They showed 4- to 7-year-olds a picture of a small rectangle divided into blue and white portions. The child's task was to decide which of two larger block models, oriented differently from the smaller rectangular picture, had the same proportion of blue and white. Even 4-year-olds recognized proportional equivalence in this task, a finding that indicates relative quantity concepts emerge early. However, Spinillo and Bryant also found a result that indicated part-part problems are especially easy: children do better when one of the choices is more than half and the other is less than half. These investigators argued that this problem was easier because children could code the relative sizes of the parts as more or less than half. That is, the model and choices might be coded as blue greater than white versus white greater than blue, a strategy based on part-part coding.

Spinillo and Bryant's results along with Piaget's suggest that part-part reasoning is a developmental precursor to part-whole reasoning. However, as Sophian and Wood (1997) argue, it is not clear that part-part relative judgments were used because whenever the relation of the parts varies, the relation of part to the whole also varies. For example, blue greater than white could also be coded as blue occupies more than half of the whole. Similarly, all of the relative quantity tasks described earlier—those involving ordinal rankings, memory for relative distance, and matching of proportions—could have been solved with either part-part or part-whole relations. In fact, infants in the experiments we reviewed previously may have performed similarly. For example, in Gao et al.'s calculation task, when infants looked longer at the incorrect amount of liquid in the tall cylinder, they may have been reacting to the change in proportion between the liquid and the container or to the relation between the full and empty parts of the container. Thus, while it is theoretically possible that part-part reasoning is used first, it may not be possible to test whether this is so in tasks that have a single subdivision of an entity.

One Whole Unit versus Multiple Whole Units Next, consider the difference between relating quantities to one whole unit versus multiple whole units. As we pointed out earlier, some cases include parts per whole, but other cases involve an ensemble of wholes in which the relations are hierarchical rather than a single entity. Existing studies indicate that these problems are more difficult than those in which a part-whole relation involves a single whole. For example, in Mix et al.'s (1999) fraction calculation study, 4-year-olds performed above chance on problems with solutions less than or equal to one circle. However, not until age 6 could children solve parallel problems with up to three whole circles.

This finding might be interpreted as support for the view that children cannot conceive of quantities between whole units because of innate limitations. Gelman (1991) and Wynn (1995) argued that the representational system available from infancy works only for discrete whole number, not for relative quantities, because these involve continuous divisions between wholes. If children have more difficulty with problems that involve solutions between whole units, isn't this consistent with the innate constraints view? We think not for two reasons. First, even though proficiency with mixed number problems emerges after proficiency with fractional problems, it still appears long before children learn conventional skills. If children are not using conventional skills to solve these problems, then the preverbal representation must be applicable to relative quantity. Second, problems with solutions less than or equal to one still require responses relative to a whole unit. Thus, the ability to solve both problem types reflects knowledge of relative quantity. The fact that mixed number problems are more difficult simply shows development in understanding of relative quantity over the early childhood period—just as in the understanding of absolute quantity.

Whole Units versus Measurement Units Now consider the case of relative quantities that involve a measurement unit but no whole per se, as for rate. Piaget (1970) found that children's conceptions of such quantities emerge rather late. Until about age 6, children treat rate problems in terms of speed alone, rather than in terms of distance, speed, and time. For example, they erroneously believe that a faster moving object will take more time to cover a space than a slower moving object covering that same space. Slightly later, at 6 to 7 years of age, children identify slower movement with more effort and more effort with greater time.

These children ignore distance differences and simply conclude that objects moving at a slower speed require more time. Not until 8 years of age and beyond can children solve rate problems correctly, so this is the latest type of relative quantity skill to emerge. Similarly, at least until age 9, children equate density with weight rather than relativizing weight per unit volume (Smith, Carey, & Wiser, 1985). Problems such as these without a whole unit are particularly difficult to solve because both the target and reference quantities constantly shift. To solve these problems, children must coordinate multiple dimensions and abstract a function that describes their interplay rather than referring to a whole unit. Whereas all proportions could be seen as functions, only proportions without whole units *must* be construed this way.

In sum, the relation between a target amount and the whole unit may affect problem difficulty. Some have argued that part-part reasoning can be used before reasoning about any relation between part and whole. This may be true, but the existing studies have failed to demonstrate it clearly because designing tasks that clearly test these approaches separately is difficult. There is some evidence that problems involving multiple wholes are more difficult than simple part-whole problems with one unit, but not necessarily because of conceptual constraints of an innate number representation. Finally, the most difficult type of relation involves no whole at all, for which children must abstract a function relating multiple dimensions.

Conclusions

In one sense, relative quantity is a primitive notion available from infancy. In fact, being able to perceptually compare full and empty portions of a container may be important or even critical to the judgment of amount of continuous quantity. However, difficulty in making relative judgments arises in certain conditions. Recognizing ordinality, relations between multiple wholes, and relations involving no whole are particularly difficult. Children also can be misled when the proportion of a target amount in a whole or set is smaller in absolute quantity but greater in relative quantity than for another whole or set. It seems to be easier for children to deal with continuous relative quantities than discrete relative quantities, at least initially. Finally, children do well when a greater number of parts corresponds to a greater relative quantity but not so well in the reverse case.

These trends offer some insight into the developmental changes that occur in early concepts of relative quantity. Some of these changes appear outside the domain of number and may therefore reflect changes in domain-general processes. For example, children can perform implicit relative quantity tasks, such as judging whether a bug will get eaten on a particular mixture of flowers and spiders, before they can make explicit comparisons. This trend has been observed in comparisons more generally, such as color groupings (see Smith, 1993). The increased number of whole units that a child can keep in mind during relative quantity tasks may be related to changes in memory. That is, as memory capacity increases, children may be able to consider where a quantity fits in relative to more than one landmark. This notion is similar to Piaget's idea that young children are unable to focus on multiple aspects of a situation (i.e., centration). Case (1985) has argued that children stop exhibiting centration as their memory improves.

Other changes in relative quantity concepts may be specific to the quantitative domain. In previous chapters, we highlighted the importance of learning to represent quantities exactly, either via a mental model or conventional counting. Once children can represent discrete number exactly, they tend to do so whenever they can. In chapter 5, we discussed Miller's (1984) work on preschool measurement in which young children sometimes used a counting strategy to divide amounts of food, even when this strategy resulted in an unfair distribution of amount (e.g., two large pieces vs. two small pieces). The impact of an exact representation of discrete number is apparent in the literature on relative quantity judgments as well. Children are much better at reasoning about changes in the target amount (i.e., the numerator) than they are about changes in the referent (i.e., denominator). This trend makes sense if children use a discrete number strategy. That is, they may be comparing counts of the target amounts without regard for the relative quantity aspect. This strategy would get them into trouble on problems in which the referent changes instead. Another example is the pattern of performance on continuous and discrete relative quantity tasks. Although children initially performed better on continuous quantity tasks, once they begin to represent discrete quantities exactly, performance with continuous amounts falls behind. Thus, the advent of an exact representation for discrete number may have ramifications for all aspects of quantitative development, including performance on tasks of relative quantity.

So far in this book, we have alluded many times to the preverbal representation of quantity. The studies we have reviewed show conclusively that infants and young children can detect and remember quantity long before they have mastered the conventional counting system. However, there is much controversy over the best way to characterize this ability. In the next chapter, we will consider the different models that have been proposed and evaluate them against the entire body of evidence representing infancy to school age.

7

Nonverbal Representation of Quantity

The preceding chapters described the quantitative skills children exhibit before they acquire conventional counting and arithmetic. Indeed, even young infants are sensitive to quantity. But how do they do it? What kind of representation are they using, if not a verbal representation?

Several models of nonverbal quantitative representation have been proposed: subitizing, the accumulator, object representations, and mental models. Of these, all but the mental models view assume that infants represent quantities in terms of discrete number. However, as we have seen, there is reason to think that infants do not represent quantities numerically at all. Instead, the evidence points to the use of overall amount. Does this mean that children do not represent discrete numbers until they have learned to count? In chapter 5, we proposed that the emergence of a nonconventional symbolic process for representing discrete number—a mental model—helps children differentiate continuous and discrete quantities. There is evidence that this representation develops before children have learned the conventional counting system. Thus, we conclude that not a single nonverbal representation of quantity but two modes of representation emerge successively (i.e., amount in infancy and discrete number in preschool).

Before we develop this account further, we will spend some time considering the other proposed models. Even though these models are not consistent with infants' use of amount, it would be premature to reject them because certain aspects of these models are still viable even if infants use overall amount. Indeed, we conclude this chapter by proposing a hybrid account that combines parts of the subitizing and object representation accounts with the mental models view. Furthermore, when the proposed models are evaluated in light of both the infant and early childhood literatures, additional issues arise that deserve consideration. To begin, we discuss the model of nonverbal quantification that was proposed first: subitizing.

Subitizing

It is a widely accepted notion that adults use two distinct processes to enumerate sets. The first, subitizing, is a rapid, accurate process of enumeration that applies exclusively to small sets. The slower, more effortful process of counting can handle large sets (Jensen, Reese, & Reese, 1950; Jevons, 1871; Kaufman, Lord, Reese, & Volkmann, 1949; Klahr, 1973; Simon & Vaishnavi, 1996; Taves, 1941; Trick & Pylyshyn, 1994).[1] This distinction is evident when one plots reaction time or accuracy for reporting the number of items in a display as a function of set size. A sharp difference in slope appears around four items.[2] As shown in figure 7.1, the slope for sets with fewer than four items is shallow, whereas the slope for sets with more than four items is steep, indicating that people use different processes to enumerate small and large sets. The same pattern of results has been found in children as young as 5 years, although they are slower to respond overall than adults (Chi & Klahr, 1975).

Subitizing is often proposed as an explanation for the performance of animals and preverbal infants on quantitative tasks (e.g., Davis, 1984; Starkey & Cooper, 1980; Trick & Pylyshyn, 1994) for two reasons. One is that both subitizing and infant performance are limited to small sets. Adults and children usually subitize up to about four items. Similarly, infants can discriminate, at most, four from three (Strauss & Curtis, 1981). This has led some to speculate that both behaviors reflect the same underlying process. The second reason is that some believe subitizing is a low-level perceptual process, perhaps a reasonable way to explain the performance of subjects who cannot use conventional counting.

1. A third enumeration process called estimation is sometimes discussed. Estimation is said to operate on extremely large sets, continuous quantities, or under conditions of limited exposure.

2. The actual point at which this discontinuity has been observed varies from three to seven items across experiments. In addition, individual differences in subitizing range are found between subjects within the same experiment (cf. Trick & Pylyshyn, 1994). The actual number of items subitized is less crucial than evidence of the discontinuity itself.

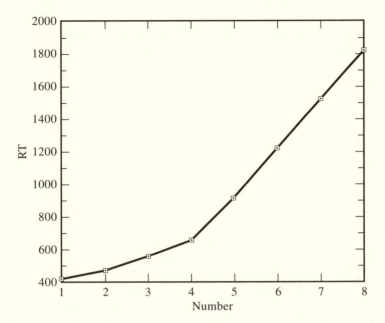

FIGURE 7.1 An idealized subitizing curve. Trick, L., and Pylyshyn, Z. (1994). Why are small and large numbers enumerated differently? A limited-capacity preattentive stage in vision. *Psychological Review*, 101, 80–102. Copyright © 1994 by the American Psychological Association. Reprinted with permission of the American Psychological Association and Dr. Lana Trick.

However, subitizing leaves a lot to be desired as an explanation because it has yet to be explained itself. There are currently several proposals. One involves recognizing canonical patterns. Mandler and Shebo (1982) noted that small sets tend to form recognizable patterns—one object is a point, two objects form a line, three objects often form a triangle, and so forth. They argued that people use these patterns to determine the cardinality of small sets. However, because pattern becomes indeterminate as sets increase beyond three items, subitizing would be limited to the smallest sets.

Mandler and Shebo (1982) found support for the pattern recognition view in a series of training studies with adults. They showed that adults could learn to rapidly apprehend the numerosity of larger sets when the sets repeatedly appeared in certain configurations. However, subsequent research has challenged the pattern recognition view. Even though pattern cues are less reliable for sets of three than for one or two, there is no significant increase in reaction time. In fact, adults can subitize linear arrays of three as quickly and accurately as triangular arrays, even though linear arrays of three should be confused with arrays of two (Trick, 1987). Also, most studies report a slope of 20 msec per item even within the subitizing range. If subjects are identifying stable patterns, there is no reason why the pattern for two should take longer to identify than the pattern for one, and so forth (Simon, 1997).

Trick and Pylyshyn (1994) proposed an alternative account of subitizing based on visuo-spatial processing. In this account, subitizing is a by-product of the preattentive individuation that occurs whenever a person visually perceives a scene. As people identify separate feature clusters, supposedly they assign to each cluster a reference token called a Finger of Instantiation or FINST. These reference tokens separate individuals and track their locations. That is, "FINSTs, like pointing fingers, provide a way of saying 'that one' without explicitly stating properties" (Trick & Pylyshyn, 1994, p. 86). However, likely only three to five FINSTs operate at any one time because this number is high enough to allow computation of spatial relations without being too costly. For example, if you can identify two individuals, you can determine whether the items are next to each other or one is in front. Because of this processing trade-off, the number of FINSTs corresponds to the subitizing range.

In support of the FINST account, Trick and Pylyshyn showed that subitizing does not occur when attention is needed to define and individuate items. For example, tracking spatial locations on a contour requires visual attention. When Trick and Pylyshyn asked adults to identify the number of items on the same contour, their reaction times were consistent with counting rather than subitizing. However, when adults were asked to identify the number of items of a certain color—a task that does not require visual attention—their reaction times were faster and more uniform across set size, indicating subitizing had occurred. This suggests that both subitizing and FINST assignment are preattentive and thus the two processes might actually be the same.

A study by Simon and Vaishnavi (1996) provides additional evidence for the FINST account. They argued that if subjects could enumerate small sets without moving their eyes to individuate the items, then subitizing happens in parallel, as specified in Trick and Pylyshyn's account. They tested this hypothesis by showing adults arrays at such a brief presentation that responses must be based on a scan of the afterimage. People cannot individuate items in an afterimage using eye movements because the whole image moves with the eye. So, if adults could enumerate sets in afterimages, they would need to use a parallel individuation process that does not require parsing with eye movements. This is just what Simon and Vaishnavi (1996) found. Adults could enumerate sets in afterimages but only when the sets contained fewer than four items. When adults tried to enumerate larger sets in afterimages, their accuracy deteriorated significantly. Thus, if subitizing is based on the assignment of place markers, these markers appear to be assigned in parallel.

The characterizations of subitizing we have reviewed so far have been restricted to sets presented all together—what Trick and Pylyshyn (1994) call "item subitizing." However, it is theoretically possible that temporally distributed sets also are subitized. Because infant and animal research sometimes uses sequential sets, theories of subitizing should account for this. VonGlasersfeld (1982) argued that both kinds of subitizing can be explained in terms of recognizing recurring configurations. According to him, simultaneously presented sets are subitized via recognition of spatial patterns much like the canonical patterns Mandler and Shebo (1982) described. Sequentially presented sets would be subitized via recognition of temporal or rhythmic patterns. Davis and Perusse (1988) have also discussed "rhythmic subitizing" as an explanation for animals' performance in sequentially presented number tasks. They illustrated this idea with the song "Deck the Halls" for which people can sing the correct number of "Fa La La's" without knowing the cardinal number of them.

Klahr's (1973) working memory account might also cover event subitizing. According to this account, one uses an ordered list of quantitative symbols to represent the first several cardinal values. Subitizing occurs when one transfers this list to working memory and scans for a match with the set to be enumerated. Although Klahr does not specifically address event subitizing, these quantitative symbols could be assigned to sequential sets much like count words can. Whether this is so depends on the nature of these symbols that have not been described in detail. For example, if the symbols are spatial pattern templates, like the canonical patterns described by Mandler and Shebo, then they would not apply to sequences.

No direct evidence confirms event subitizing in adults. Of course, studies on frequency estimation provide abundant evidence that both children and adults can judge the number of items in a sequentially presented set with remarkable accuracy (Goldstein, Hasher, & Stein, 1983; Hasher & Chromiak, 1977; Hasher & Zacks, 1979, 1984). However, these findings are not directly related to event subitizing and the link between these two areas is still unclear. The design of frequency estimation tasks does not lend itself easily to this comparison. Subjects in frequency estimation experiments typically report how many times they have seen a particular item randomly presented several times in a long series of words or pictures. Clearly, this is not the most direct way to test event subitizing as the authors we cited have characterized it. However, future work might explore a possible connection between these literatures.

How well can subitizing explain the performance of young children and infants on nonverbal numerical tasks? The answer to this question depends on the characterization of subitizing one accepts. The item subitizing accounts, especially Trick and Pylyshyn's, seem to have the strongest empirical support, at least in studies of adults. However, because FINSTs are assigned in parallel as part of spatial individuation, it is not obvious how they could be used on sequential tasks. Wynn (1996) found that infants could discriminate between different sets of puppet jumps. If FINSTs are assigned all at once, how could they track these events? Trick and Pylyshyn themselves caution that their account is specific to static visual scenes. Therefore, this account does not readily explain the results of experiments involving sequential presentation (Canfield & Smith, 1996; Mix, 1999a; Wynn, 1996), including the nonverbal calculation studies (Huttenlocher et al., 1994; Simon et al., 1995; Wynn, 1992). Theoretically, event subitizing could be used in these contexts. For example, infants might respond in Wynn's experiment on the basis of rhythmic pattern matching. However, more work is needed to specify the processes underlying event subitizing in a way that can be tested. Furthermore, new evidence discussed in chapter 2 suggests infants attend to continuous quantity rather than discrete number (Clearfield & Mix, 1999; Feigenson & Spelke, 1998) as shown in both number discrimination studies and calculation studies. If so, then item individuation would be unrelated to performance in these tasks.

Subitizing may have been adopted too quickly as a developmental explanation. As we have noted, the only direct link between subitizing and early quantitative development is the set sizes that can be processed. The subitizing range is around one to four items. Similarly, infants and young children can perform quantitative tasks for only small sets. However, this link may be coincidental. The processing limitations that affect performance in infants and young children may be quite different from those that set the subitizing range in adults. For example, the set size limits for infants might reflect changes in proportion as set sizes increase. That is, the proportional difference between one and two items is much greater than the proportional difference between four and five items.

The Accumulator

Imagine that you were keeping track of the number of sheep jumping a fence. But instead of counting the sheep verbally, you poured a cup of water into a cylinder for each one. The total set of sheep would be represented by how full the cylinder became. You could use the cylinder to make comparisons. For example, you could compare the fullness of the cylinder today with the fullness of the cylinder yesterday to determine whether you lost any sheep. Now, imagine that instead of sheep, you wanted to measure how long it took the sheep to move from one pasture to another. You could use the same cylinder in a different way; you could pour water into the cylinder at a constant rate until all the sheep had moved. The resulting fullness of the cylinder would represent the total duration.

This example illustrates how the accumulator mechanism works. Meck and Church (1983) proposed this mechanism to account for the timing and counting behavior they observed in rats. In their study, they presented sequential sets of light flashes or tones and trained the rats to press a lever on one side for a large set (eight events) and on the other side for a small set (two events). During the training trials, number and duration covaried so that the eight event sequences also took longer to present than the two event sequences. At test, the rats were presented with sequences of four—either four events that varied in total duration or a variable number of events that lasted four seconds in duration. Meck and Church found that the rats spontaneously generalized in both test conditions (see figure 7.2). If duration varied, they pressed the lever that corresponded to longer or shorter durations. If number varied, they pressed the lever that corresponded to higher or lower numbers. Interestingly, rats trained on one mode readily transferred to the other mode at test. That is, a rat trained to discriminate on the basis of duration would immediately generalize to test trials that differed in number. Furthermore, when amphetamines were administered before the test trials—a manipulation that had caused underestimates of duration in previous research—rats underestimated on both the duration and number trials to the same extent. Meck and Church concluded that animals use the same mechanism for timing and counting: the accumulator.

This mechanism works by using an endogenous pacemaker to emit pulses at a constant rate (see figure 7.3). To begin timing or counting, a switch is closed that gates pulses into a container. If the accumulator is counting, the switch gates in pulses one at a time. If the accumulator is timing, the switch stays open until timing has stopped. The resulting fullness of the container represents the total quantity or duration, depending on which mode has been operated.

The accumulator has been coopted by several investigators as an explanation for the performance of infants and children on quantitative tasks. However, their conclusions about later development vary. In the preverbal counting view, the accumulator is thought to operate much like verbal counting (Gallistel & Gelman, 1992) because it seems to obey the principles of verbal counting described by Gelman and Gallistel (1978).[3] For example, in verbal counting, each count word can be

3. These principles are described briefly here. For a more detailed discussion, see chapter 8.

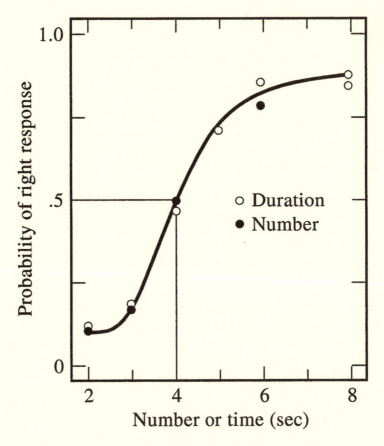

FIGURE 7.2 Psychophysical function for duration and number for rats in Meck and Church's 1983 experiment. Meck, W. H., and Church, R. M. (1983). A mode control model of counting and timing processes. *Journal of Experimental Psychology: Animal Behavior Processes*, 9, 320–324. Copyright © 1983 by the American Psychological Association. Reprinted with permission.

assigned to one, and only one, item in a set. Similarly, Gallistel and Gelman argue, each gating of pulses into the accumulator corresponds to only one item to be counted. In verbal counting, the linguistic tags must be used in a consistent sequence to be meaningful. Similarly, the accumulator produces representations of magnitude that order by size. Finally, the last word in a verbal count stands for the numerosity of the set. With the accumulator, the final *magnitude* stands for the numerosity of the set. Because of these parallels, Gallistel and Gelman contend that the accumulator constitutes a legitimate counting system.

This conclusion has important developmental implications. Because

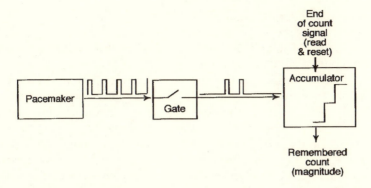

FIGURE 7.3 Graphic depection of Meck and Church's (1983) accumulator model. Reprinted from *Cognition*, Vol 44, Gallistel, C. R., and Gelman, R., "Preverbal and verbal counting and computation," Pages 43–74, Copyright 1992, with permission of Elsevier Science and C. R. Gallistel.

Gallistel and Gelman consider preverbal and verbal counting to be isomorphic, they have argued that children should have a relatively easy time learning to count verbally. They see the accumulator as the source of implicit guiding principles—a framework that helps children make sense of the otherwise opaque conventional counting system. Thus, even before children start to count verbally, they understand the rules of counting based on their years of experience applying the accumulator. In this view, learning to count is a straightforward matter of mapping the linguistic tags (count words) onto their preverbal referents (the magnitudes produced by the accumulator).

Wynn (1995) has developed an alternative view based on the accumulator. Although she agrees that the accumulator underlies infant and early childhood quantitative abilities, she argues that mapping the linguistic tags onto the accumulator representations is a lengthy and complex process because the verbal and preverbal representations are inherently *different*. The main difference, according to Wynn, is that the magnitudes produced by the accumulator embody ordinal relations explicitly, whereas number words derive their ordinal meaning solely from their positions relative to one another in the counting sequence. Before children can map the count words onto the accumulator values, they must first unlock the ordinal structure of the count word sequence, but this, she maintains, takes time.

In support of this interpretation, Wynn reports the results of several studies showing that learning to count is protracted and difficult (Wynn, 1990, 1992). Indeed, she has shown that children need at least one year after they have learned to recite the count words before they can understand how counting determines cardinality. In other words, even after children have memorized the count word list, they cannot yet understand the words' meaning. Wynn argues that children accomplish this by mapping the positional relations of the count words onto the magnitudinal relations of the accumulator output.

How does the accumulator fare as an account of early number development? In some ways, one can easily imagine how this mechanism could produce many of the skills infants and young children demonstrate because it is so much like verbal counting. One of the strengths of the accumulator explanation is that it can easily account for performance on sequential tasks. For example, infants could habituate to sets of puppet jumps by filling their accumulators once for each jump. Over time, they might slowly lose interest if the resulting accumulator values are the same on every trial. Similarly, children could add by accumulating the first term of the problem and then gating more units in each time new items are added.

Proponents of the accumulator account can also explain the set size limits observed in infant and early childhood number research (Gallistel & Gelman, 1992; Wynn, 1995). They argue that the accumulator is inherently inexact because of variability in the rate of the pulses and the duration of the gate closings. This error would be normally distributed around the true value. So infants habituated to sets of three might represent one display as two, the next display as four, and so forth.[4] Because of more room for error at higher numerosities, performance should become less reliable as numerosity increases. Indeed, when rats are taught to produce a specific number of bar presses, the distributions of their responses flatten as number increases, although at numerosities much higher than infants can discriminate (e.g., Mechner, 1958).

Nonetheless, even though the accumulator can explain some facts of quantitative development, it fails under other evidence. First, consider habituation to static visual sets. Seemingly, it would be difficult for infants to keep track of which items in a visual set had been "accumulated" without physically partitioning the set, as we do in verbal counting. Even if enumerating static sets with an accumulator is possible, it should be more difficult than enumerating sequential sets. However, just the opposite trend appears in preschool children (Mix, 1999a; Schaeffer, Eggleston, & Scott, 1974). In infants, only preliminary evidence suggests any sensitivity to quantity in sequentially presented sets and certainly nothing suggests that sequential sets are easier.

The accumulator also cannot explain infants' apparent use of overall amount rather than discrete number in quantitative tasks (Clearfield & Mix, 1999; Feigenson & Spelke, 1998). The accumulator can enumerate sets of discrete events, or it can measure continuous amount of

---

4. Note that this is similar to the argument Huttenlocher et al. (1994) made regarding the exactness of infant representations of number.

time. In sequential sets, it is clear that rats at least can move back and forth between these two types of quantity. But for a static visual set, how could the accumulator measure continuous quantity? Perhaps it could measure duration as individual items are scanned, but the scans must be carried out smoothly and at a constant rate. No one has demonstrated, or even suggested, that the accumulator can operate this way. In fact, if it could, why would the counting mode be necessary?

A third problem is that many empirical findings cannot be explained without positing complicated maneuvers involving multiple accumulators. For example, consider Wynn's (1995) description of how the accumulator could be used to solve a subtraction problem. "Suppose accumulator A represents the initial value, and accumulator B, the value to be subtracted. Successively removing increments of the contents of A— or to avoid loss of information of the initial value of A, the contents of A′, a copy of A—and 'pouring' them into an initially empty accumulator C until C reaches the same fullness as B (indicating the right amount has been removed) would result in A′ representing the difference between the values represented by A and B" (p. 51). This solution requires four accumulators and works only on the assumption that pulses can be gated *out*. Although this is logically possible, no one has specified how many accumulators an individual can maintain at one time or whether pulses in an accumulator retain their individuality so that they can be gated out separately. In short, whereas the accumulator as originally described can explain some behaviors, it cannot account for others without modification and added complexity.

There are also more basic problems. For example, how can such a mechanism ever produce a representation of cardinal number? Although the count words derive their meaning in part from their position in the count word list, it is possible to represent cardinality without ordinality (e.g., Russell, 1919/1993). For example, one can map the word "three" onto a set of three things without knowing that three is less than four, similar to knowing that "blue" is blue without knowing that it falls between green and violet in the spectrum. The accumulator cannot capture this aspect of number because an accumulator value is meaningful only when it is compared to another accumulator value. For instance, you could order different lengths of rope, but the individual length would not have a cardinal value, unless either (1) it was in a container of finite length so that the proportion of fullness to emptiness could be used or (2) it could be parsed into units, as with a ruler. As we argued before, subdividing existing accumulator magnitudes this way may not be possible.

Finally, there is no direct evidence for the accumulator mechanism in infants and children. The accumulator was proposed as a model that might explain the behavior of rats and was extended to developmental research because neither infants, young children, nor rats can use conventional verbal skills to do quantitative tasks. The thinking was that if this mechanism had evolved for use in lower animals like rats, probably we humans also have it. Yet nothing in the early number literature suggests that this is the case. An important aspect of the accumulator model that distinguishes it from others is its emphasis on ordinality. As Simon (1997) points out, there is no evidence that infants recognize ordinal relations. The only hint that they can comes from Cooper's (1984) work with infants who were already more than a year old. Furthermore, as we argued, it should be easier to use the accumulator on sequential sets rather than static sets when physical partitioning cannot be used. The accumulator, like verbal counting, requires that the set be partitioned as it is enumerated. That is, tagged items must be separated from items yet to be tagged. In verbal counting, people accomplish this by moving or touching items as they are tagged. In experimental tasks that do not allow infants or children to touch the items, sequential presentation would accomplish the same end. However, the evidence suggests that tasks involving sequential sets are actually as difficult or more so for infants and young children than those involving static sets.

Like the subitizing accounts, the accumulator may have been accepted too quickly as a developmental account based on similarities between infants and animals that could be coincidental. In fact, there are important differences in the kinds of evidence obtained for infants and animals. Animals usually make active responses in the form of lever presses or searches for treats in particular locations, whereas infant studies have relied on passive responses, such as looking preference. Animal subjects are most often highly trained adults, whereas infants obviously are not. Animal experiments have tested numerosities as high as 24, whereas infant discriminations have been limited almost exclusively to very small sets. Finally, although there is now evidence that infants can detect differences in sequential sets, no one has shown in infants what Meck and Church (1983) showed in rats: they can generalize a response for a sequential set in one modality, to an equivalent set in another modality, regardless of variations in duration. In short, animal experiments seem to provide a more rigorous test of the accumulator than the existing infant studies. Although infants might possess a quantitative ability similar to that found in animals, it remains to be demonstrated. Another possibility is that the accumulator fits the animal data better because what infants do is fundamentally different from what rats do.

Object Representation Accounts

Now imagine that you are counting the same sheep as before, but this time you point a stick toward each sheep in the herd. If one of the sheep moves, you change the direction of the stick to follow it. Once you're finished counting, the set of sticks would stand for the set of sheep. If you wanted to compare your herd to the neighbor's, you could take your sticks over and match them with each of his sheep in one-to-one correspondence. Keeping the sticks pointed at the right sheep would get more difficult as the number of sheep increased. In fact, you might be able to keep track of only three or four sheep at a time this way. This is the idea behind object representation explanations of early number performance.

These explanations involve assigning an abstract token to each individual in a set. Such accounts are based on hypothesized processes of spatial individuation in adults that have also been used to explain item subitizing, as we discussed. When people perceive a visual scene, they encode both what objects are there and where the objects are located. The "where" system is faster and operates preattentively. This system encodes spatial location but does not add details about object features or identity. These details come later as the attentional mechanisms of the "what" system take over. It is the object individuation process of the where system that has been coopted by number researchers.

This individuation process has been characterized two ways. The first involves the formation of "object files" (Kahneman, Treisman, & Gibbs, 1992), when an object is first perceived. Initially the stored information is limited to location, but later it may also include features or a verbal label if the object is identified. The information in an object file is continually updated as the object moves or otherwise changes. The file stays intact as long as the object is visible and during brief occlusions. However, if the spatio-temporal continuity is sufficiently interrupted, the object file will be discarded.

Spatial individuation has been characterized also in Trick and Pylyshyn's (1994) FINST hypothesis, described in greater detail earlier. As noted before, FINST tokens are assigned like pointing fingers. These fingers are assigned in parallel, but they can track an object as it moves through space. The object file and FINST ideas are similar in many ways. In fact, one might think of a FINST as an object file that has just been assigned and contains only location information.

These spatial individuation models have been adopted by researchers who examine early numerical ability (Simon, 1997; Uller et al., 1999). Simon proposed that infants respond in quantitative tasks by creating tokens to represent each object in a set. To establish equivalence, Simon posits that infants compare the remembered tokens with the items in a visible scene using one-to-one correspondence (see figure 7.4). For example, consider Wynn's (1992) calculation experiment. Infants see an object and then a screen is raised. Then a second object goes behind the screen. When the screen is lowered, infants look longer when there is one object rather than two. According to Simon,

FIGURE 7.4 Simon's object file explanation of Wynn's (1992) infant calculation results. Reprinted from *Cognitive Development*, Vol 12, Simon, T. J., "Reconceptualizing the origins of number knowledge: A 'non-numerical' account." Pages 349–372, Copyright 1997, with permission of Elsevier Science and T. J. Simon.

when the first object is presented, infants assign a token to it. When the second object is presented, they assign a second token. When the screen is lowered, infants match their mental tokens to the visible objects and may be surprised to find that the number of tokens exceeds the number of objects (or vice versa). Simon calls this account "nonnumerical" because it requires only domain-general mechanisms that are not evolved especially for numerical processing. Furthermore, he does not consider the object token representations to be cardinal because no single symbol stands for the numerosity of the entire set. Instead, the object tokens together form a symbolic analogue of the actual set.

Uller, Carey, Huntley-Fenner, and Klatt (1999) have proposed a similar account. But Uller et al. add an imagistic component. They argue that infants create an imagistic model of the entire scene—not just abstract tokens for the objects. Furthermore, Uller et al. consider this representation to be numerical because it requires some criterion for numerical identity. In other words, you need a way to tell whether you're seeing the same thing twice or two different things. Moreover, Uller et al. argue that the use of one-to-one correspondence process implies genuinely numerical processing.

In support of their imagistic account, Uller et al. (1999) presented evidence that experimental manipulations that would affect the formation of such a model also affect infants' performance in Wynn's (1992) calculation task. For example, in Wynn's procedure, infants see an object, it is screened, and then a second object is added. Uller et al. showed that infants perform randomly in this task when the screen is presented *first* and then both objects are placed behind it one by one. They argued that it is more difficult to form an image of an object behind the screen without first seeing the object in its final destination. This experiment is not just a test of whether infants are assigning object tokens because simply assigning an object token would not depend on seeing the object in a particular location. Instead, this procedure intended to test whether infants form an image of the entire scene.

The object representation accounts have many strengths as developmental explanations. They are parsimonious. Rather than positing the existence of a complicated domain-specific knowledge structure, these accounts build on a general-purpose mechanism known to operate in adults. They also can explain most of the developmental data, including set size limits, reasonably well. Certain aspects of these accounts are not completely clear, though, and some modifications may be needed. One problem is that, if object tokens are assigned in parallel as people parse a visual scene, then how do they apply to sequences? For example, in the infant calculation experiments, object tokens would have to be assigned or discarded sequentially as objects were added or subtracted. A second problem concerns the abstractness of the tokens. Simon (1997) argued that object tokens are abstract because they are assigned to spatial locations before any other information has been gathered. Thus, when the pointers are initially assigned, they would be impoverished. However, once attention is focused and feature information is added, object tokens should become less abstract. How can these tokens omit featural information and thereby remain abstract in quantitative situations? This issue has not been addressed in the current proposals. Finally, as with the accumulator and subitizing accounts, assuming that infants represent quantities in terms of discrete individuals may be incorrect, given the recent evidence that infants respond to changes in overall amount rather than number.

Although parsimonious in comparison to other accounts, object representation accounts still build quite a lot into the infant. They claim that infants can assign symbolic tokens to objects and compare a set of internal symbols with an external display using one-to-one correspondence. But it isn't obvious that infants can assign and manipulate symbols like this. Even if these symbols are assigned automatically as the infant's "where" system parses a scene, does the infant's "where" system operate according to the same principles as the adult's? In particular, several studies have demonstrated that infants rely heavily on movement cues to see objects as separate individuals (Kellman & Spelke, 1983; Xu & Carey, 1996). Differences in appearance that adults might use, such as color, texture, or shape, are not sufficient for infants in the absence of movement cues. Because nearly all the stimuli in infant number experiments are static displays of dots or photographs, infants may not perceive these in terms of distinct individuals in the first place.

Mental Models

Huttenlocher, Jordan, and Levine (1994) posited the existence of a nonconventional symbolic process, or mental model, that can be used in quantitative tasks. They developed this account to explain children's performance on nonverbal calculation problems that we described in detail in chapter 3. Briefly, in these problems, children saw a set of blocks and then these were hidden underneath a cover. Then the hidden set was transformed by either adding or removing blocks. Children's task was to lay out a set of blocks equivalent to the hidden set after the transformation. Children began to produce precise, accurate responses to such problems around 3 years of age—years earlier than children can solve the same problems stated in words or in story problems (Huttenlocher, Jordan, & Levine, 1994; Levine, Jordan, & Huttenlocher, 1992).

Huttenlocher et al. proposed that children do this by constructing a mental version of the hidden set—a mental model—and imagining items moving in or out of the set. The mental model explicitly represents features of the situation critical for calculation, such as the number of countable entities in the initial set and the nature of the transformation, but does not preserve task-irrelevant features, such as the color of the individual items or their spatial arrangement. Huttenlocher et al. hypothesized that the ability to form these mental models emerges in early childhood about the same time that other symbolic abilities develop, such as language, model use, and pretend play.

The mental models view has several similarities with the object representation accounts. Both involve assigning a token to each item in a set so that the total number is represented by the group of tokens. Just as object representation accounts hold that these tokens can follow items as they move through space, the symbols in a mental model can be moved to recreate the movement of the items they represent. Are these accounts based on the same representation? If so, does this representation underlie subitizing, as some have claimed? We will explore this intriguing possibility in a moment. But first, there are some important differences between these views to keep in mind.

First, mental models are more than by-products of visual processing. They consist of symbols that can be assigned sequentially, moved through mental space, added, or subtracted. Ideally, these symbols include only task-relevant information, but, in principle, they can include any available featural information. Thus, they might contain spatial information if it is relevant to some task, but they are not simply spatial pointers.

Second, whereas the object representation accounts attribute an exact representation of number to infants, Huttenlocher et al. (1994) linked the emergence of mental models to advances in symbolic development (e.g., pretend play, word learning, etc.) that occur in early childhood. Therefore, the use of mental models is an intermediate step between infants' initial quantitative awareness and the subsequent acquisition of conventional skills. The evidence for this is that children under 3 years in the nonverbal calculation task give incorrect answers that approximate the correct solution. Because a mental model, by definition, would provide an exact representation, the approximate responses of younger children have been attributed to their inexact memories without a mental model. Given that infants also respond approximately in quantitative tasks, there is no reason to credit them with a mental model either.

A third difference is that the symbols in a mental model begin as detailed representations of the actual items that gradually become more sparse. Depending on the situation and the task at hand, certain features will be preserved, whereas others will be discarded. Thus, the symbols in a mental model become more abstract as irrelevant information is shed. In contrast, object files or FINSTs are initially impoverished and become more detailed as the "what" system incorporates featural information. This initial lack of information has been taken to mean that these tokens are also abstract (Simon, 1997). However, this "abstraction" is based on a brief period before information is perceived. As this information is added, object representations should become less abstract.

Because of this, the mental models account provides a better explanation for the data on children's recognition of numerical equivalence. In chapter 3, we discussed the finding that children recognize equivalence between a hidden set and one of two choice arrays more easily if the surface similarity between the equivalent sets is high (Mix, 1999b). For example, it is easier to recognize that two black disks are equal to two black dots than it is to recognize that an eraser and a penny are equal to two black dots. If children represented the hidden sets with abstract pointers, one condition should not be easier than the other. However, these findings are easily interpreted within the mental models framework because the symbols might start with extraneous details. If children are not yet proficient at identifying or eliminating unnecessary detail, then surface features could affect performance even in a memory task.

Let's return to the question of how mental models, object representations, and subitizing might be related. The mental models described by Huttenlocher et al. (1994) might originate from the kind of spatial individuation processes coopted in the object representation accounts (i.e., FINSTs and object files). That does not mean that infants would use these processes in quantitative tasks. They might use them only to differentiate objects in a scene. In fact, we believe that it takes children several years to use these processes as abstract, numerical representations. During this time, we posit a progressive change in the object-based representation, as well as how quantitative situations are generally viewed.

Consider the following scenario. Perhaps infants are born with or quickly develop a "where" system of spatial pointers. At first, these pointers are assigned only when movement cues suggest that two objects are distinct. Because they are assigned in parallel, they would apply only to objects present simultaneously. The pointers would not apply to events or sounds, given that these entities are usually sequential and rarely spatially distinct (unless the objects related to the events are also spatially distinct, as with multiple birds singing in different trees).

Within a particular instance, the "what" system would become active soon after the pointers were assigned, and additional object features would be incorporated. Habituation studies have shown that infants are sensitive to differences in color, shape, and so forth (see Kellman & Banks, 1998, for a review). Even though infants may not use distinctive features to tell objects apart until their first birthdays (Xu & Carey, 1996), they are aware of these features and could incorporate them into their object representations. As infants learn more about object features, their object representations should become richer and even more detailed.

During this period, infants would not use these pointers in quantitative situations. There would be no need to do so. In almost all situations, they could use estimates of overall amount instead (Clearfield & Mix, 1999; Feigenson & Spelke, 1998; Gao et al., 2000; Newcombe et al., 1999). For example, the first author's son, Spencer, for several months toward the middle of his first year was fascinated by people eating. He seemed shocked to see food go into someone's mouth and disappear. During these episodes, Spencer may have been learning that eating causes the quantity of food on a person's plate to decrease. However, even if the food were in discrete pieces (e.g., separate cookies), he could have noted the change without knowing the number of pieces. Instead, he could have estimated the amount of food space relative to the empty plate space.

Children might continue to use overall amount for several years. Huttenlocher et al.'s (1994) finding that 2-year-olds generate approximate responses in the nonverbal calculation task means that children may still use overall amount at that age (although they might also use an inaccurate version of the mental model, i.e., approximate number). Either way, children would eventually discover that they can use their familiar pointers in a new way—to compare sets. This process might require the development of several new abilities: increased memory capacity to sustain multiple object representations over time, the ability to manipulate object representations in mental space, and so forth.

The evidence suggests that children acquire these requisite abilities and start to use a mental model to perform quantitative tasks close to their third birthdays (Huttenlocher et al., 1994). Because the symbols in this model would be grounded in object individuation, they would not readily apply to event sets, as Mix (1999a) found. Furthermore, children might not know which features of these representations were irrelevant until they had learned more about numerical tasks. For this reason, they might show surface similarity effects in memory tasks for many months (Mix, 1999b). As the symbols in the mental model are being tailored to numerical tasks, children would be mastering the conventional counting system. As we will see in chapter 8, the mental model representation could provide conceptual referents for the first few count words. As such, the use of these representations might also underlie the subitizing phenomenon, as others have suggested (Simon, 1997; Trick & Pylyshyn, 1994). That is, if the first few number names become strongly associated with different mental models (derived from sets of spatial individuation markers), then these associations might underlie the subitizing pattern in older children and adults.

In summary, the scenario we have proposed here incorporates both object representation and mental models to explain the data across infancy and early childhood. Admittedly, this scenario is speculative and has not been tested directly. Still, of the current proposals, it provides the best fit to the extant data. In chapter 8, we will consider how conventional skills are mapped onto preexisting quantitative representations. Based on the present evaluation, we will take the mental models view as our starting point.

8

Acquiring Conventional Skills

As we have seen, infants and young children begin processing quantitative information well before they acquire mathematical conventions. However, mastery of conventional symbols may be necessary for mathematical thinking beyond a certain point, and eventually children do learn conventional skills. In this chapter, we consider how these skills, including counting, whole number calculation, measurement, and fraction notation, are acquired.

The mastery of conventional skills is a complex process that lasts through the entire childhood period and beyond. To appreciate the complexity involved, consider that just learning whole number calculation conventions usually involves learning strategies such as counting-on, memorizing simple number facts (e.g., 2 + 2 = 4), understanding base-ten structure, learning the processes of borrowing and carrying, and more. In fact, entire books have been written about the acquisition of single conventional skills. We do not attempt to capture all the details of conventional symbol acquisition in this chapter. Instead, we focus on the earliest achievements and how conventions might map onto preexisting representations.

Various relations can exist between mathematical conventions and the concepts they encode. Mathematical conventions can be mapped directly onto preexisting concepts. Gelman (1991) has claimed that this is what happens in learning the count words. However, learners may acquire other mathematical notions without preexisting concepts. For example, students may learn about exponents in school without having any informal knowledge of them. In fact, learning conventions may itself act as the catalyst for some conceptual changes. Certain conventions may be acquired without producing mathematical understandings at all. In other words, they may be used for some period of time in a rote fashion. For example, a child could memorize multiplication facts, such as "9 × 9 = 81," without understanding that they encode the successive addition of equal sets. As we will see, all of these relations are evident in children's early acquisition of mathematical conventions. We begin by considering how conventional counting systems are acquired.

Counting

What Are Counting Systems?

Counting is used to determine the precise cardinal numerosity of a set—information that is important for many purposes. I just took 41 ears of your corn, so that is how many I must give back next week. There are 23 children in my class, so that is the number of class t-shirts I need to buy. The usefulness of a counting system depends on certain characteristics. There is little room for variation in these characteristics if counting is to serve its purpose.

Gelman and Gallistel (1978) identified five principles that counting systems must follow to be useful. Three of these specify "how to count." The one-to-one principle implies that every item in a display should be tagged with one unique counting tag. So, if someone counts four items, "one-two-two-three," the result will be wrong. It also will be wrong if the person skips an item in the set or assigns two tags to the same item. The stable order principle stipulates that the counting tags maintain a consistent sequence. The counting sequence consists of arbitrary symbols. Its meaning derives from being in a consistent order. If counting tags were used in a different order every time, then the last tag used would have no particular significance. The third "how to count" principle—cardinality—holds that the final tag used in a count represents the total numerosity of the set. If someone counts to 2,000 following the stable order and one-to-one principles, he can be assured that the set contains 2,000 items.

The remaining two principles specify "what to count." The abstraction principle states that any combination of discrete entities can be counted. So one can count the family pets, a series of sneezes, or a grouping that includes a star, a memory, and a rock. Of course, there must be some reason to group items together before counting them.

That is, numerosity applies to a class or category chosen in advance. However, as long as an entity can be individuated, it can be counted. Finally, the order irrelevance principle refers to the fact that items in a set may be tagged in any order, as long as the other counting principles are not violated. One can count a row beginning on the left, the right, the center out, the ends in; the same cardinal value is reached as long as each item is tagged once and only once.

As long as one follows these five principles, any counting system will work, no matter how unconventional it may seem on the surface. In English-speaking countries we tag each item with a count word and then use the last count word to stand for the numerosity of the set. This linguistic tagging procedure is used in other cultures as well, but with the count words of that language (e.g., "un, deux, trois"). Nonlinguistic tagging procedures also are possible. For example, some aboriginal groups assign body parts to each item in a count (see Dehaene, 1997, or Nunes & Bryant, 1996, for a discussion). Some cultures, such as the Warlpiris tribe in Australia, have very few tags, just enough for two or three items (Dixon, 1980). Another difference among counting systems is the embodiment of a base structure. Some counting systems, such as those based on body parts, use no base structure at all. Others use a base-ten structure but vary in how transparently this structure is reflected in the tags. For example, the underlying base-ten place-value structure of the Hindu-Arabic number system is less transparent in the English words "eleven" and "twelve" than it is in their Chinese counterparts that translate "ten-one" and "ten-two" (Miller & Stigler, 1987). However, despite these crosscultural variations, all counting systems adhere to the same counting principles.

Some have argued that counting systems share these universal characteristics because enumeration is an evolutionarily selected, innate endowment of all human beings (Starkey et al., 1990). However, these commonalities could exist for reasons other than an innately specified structure in the brain. Counting serves a function that itself is highly constrained. If you want to trade 40 ears of corn for 6 chickens, you need an enumeration system with all of the properties Gelman and Gallistel (1978) described. It must tag items once and only once. The last tag must stand for the cardinality of the set. The tags must be applicable to any set of items in any order, and so forth. The need for precision in socio-economic situations necessarily limits the amount of variability in counting systems. In other domains, such as space, greater cross-cultural variation in terminology appears (e.g., Choi & Bowerman, 1991; Danzig, 1967). However, this does not necessarily imply that space is less innately specified in the nervous system than number. It could simply mean that there are fewer constraints on the way a space can be described than there are on the way a set can be counted.

Learning to Count

Almost from the time children begin to speak, the conventional count words are part of their vocabularies (Fuson, 1988). However, these early uses of count words are disconnected from the counting act. When children first say the count words in a list, they produce them as an "inseparable chain" without regard for one-to-one correspondence (Fuson, 1988). For example, when prompted to count, they might say, "onetwothreefourfive," as if these five tags were one word. We have observed this informally in our own research. When we have asked 2- and 3-year-olds to count a row of objects, it is not uncommon for them to pass their hand over the entire set while saying count words in rapid succession. Within several months to a year, children begin to separate individual words, making it possible for them to tag items individually.

In addition to using inseparable chains, children often order their early count word sequences incorrectly. For example, a child might count five things as "one, three, six, two, four." However, these idiosyncratic lists often obey the stable order principle (Baroody & Price, 1983; Fuson, 1988; Gelman & Gallistel, 1978). That is, a child who counts, "one, three, six, two, four" will almost always count in that order. Children who use idiosyncratic lists sometimes also demonstrate understanding of cardinality (Gelman & Gallistel, 1978). For example, when asked "how many," the child who counts five things using the above list might say "four." Even though the answer is technically in error, it shows that such children understand a basic mechanism of counting: the last count word tells you how many things there are.

From the earliest stages of counting system acquisition, children seem to recognize that the count words fulfill a specific function. They rarely incorporate other tags, such as letters of the alphabet, into their count word sequences even at the continuous string level (Fuson, 1988; Gelman & Gallistel, 1978). They also understand that all count words refer to a unique quantity, even if they do not know the referents for specific words. Wynn (1992) gave 2½- to 3-year-old children two counting tasks. In one, children were asked to produce a specific set (e.g., "Give me three dinosaurs"). In the other, they were asked to point to one of two cards that showed a specific set (e.g., "Can you show me the three flowers?"). Wynn found that if children knew the cardinal meaning of a count word, such as "two," they would both produce the correct set and point it out. However, even if they could not produce a set for another count word, such as "three," they would point to three if it were paired with two. In other words, children knew that "three" referred to a numerical set that was not "two," even if they did not know the exact referent.

Of course, irrespective of age, this knowledge is evident only after children have established the meaning of at least one count word. So how do children accomplish this? Research indicates that they attach meanings to the count words one at a time, starting with those for the smallest sets. These seem to be direct mappings between number words and quantities that do not require counting. First, young children can respond in small number tasks without counting. For example, they can tell how many items are in a set of two or three without counting (Schaeffer et al., 1974). Children also respond to requests for small sets without counting the items (e.g., "Give me two blocks") (Wynn, 1990, 1992). There is a consistent ordering in this production task in which children are first able to make sets of one, then sets of two, and finally sets of three. Thus, the mappings are made one by one, rather than all at once, as one might expect if this process were linked to a sudden insight into the meaning of counting. In fact, when asked how many items were in larger sets, children in these studies did not know to respond with the last word of the count. Thus, children had mapped the small number words to their referents without understanding the function of counting.

Eventually, children discover the connection between counting and cardinality. Of the several views about how this happens, most agree that it involves making comparisons between the outcomes of different quantification processes. For example, Klahr and Wallace (1976) posited that children compare the outcomes of subitizing and counting. That is, they perceive the numerosity of a small set and label it. Eventually, they recognize that the label they give the set is the same as the last word they say in a count. Similarly, Schaeffer et al. (1974) proposed that children discover this connection by comparing the outcomes of matching and counting. Thus, a child might notice that two equivalent sets also end up with the same word in a count. On either account, children are building upon some informal sense of cardinality. In the next section, we consider in greater depth how this building might occur.

Mapping Verbal Counting onto Nonverbal Quantification

As we discussed in chapter 7, there is disagreement about how to characterize the quantification of infants and children. However, the shared assumption underlying all the proposed models is that there is a non verbal means of representing quantity. If so, then when children learn the count words, they probably make a mapping between these tags and their preexisting representations. These representations may therefore influence how the count words are acquired; learning to count may be easy or difficult depending on the way number is represented preverbally. Although only limited data relate to these issues, we review some well-developed theoretical positions organized around two main issues. The first is whether children understand the counting principles before or after they have learned to count. The second is whether preverbal quantification helps or hinders the acquisition of conventional skills.

Principles Before versus Principles After A point of debate among researchers is *when* understanding of the counting principles appears relative to acquisition of the verbal counting system. Advocates of the principles-before view argue that children understand the counting principles before they have learned to count conventionally. This idea may seem strange. How can children understand how to count before they can count? Isn't being able to count and understanding the counting principles the same thing? Although these principles certainly are embodied in conventional counting, proponents of this view argue that they also are embodied in nonverbal enumeration procedures. Thus, children may understand the basic ideas underlying verbal counting before they have been exposed to the conventional system. In fact, these investigators claim that knowledge of the counting principles helps children learn the conventional counting system, as if the principles were a skeletal structure that children flesh out with the details of their culture-specific counting system (Gallistel & Meck, 1983; Gelman & Gelman, 1992).

One finding cited in favor of the principles-before view is that children adhere to the counting principles even before they possess the skill needed to demonstrate these principles through accurate counts. The evidence reviewed before about children's use of idiosyncratic counting sequences is often cited. Specifically, the observation that children act in accordance with the "how to count" principles even when they use idiosyncratic sequences suggests that an understanding of these principles does not depend on conventional counting skill. Similar reasoning underlies a series of studies in which preschool children were asked to judge the accuracy of counts performed by a puppet (Gelman & Meck, 1983). Children detected violations of the one-to-one and stable order principles but did not object to "pseudo-errors," such as beginning a count in the middle of an array. The ability to recognize violations of the counting principles was not attributable to mastery of the conventional counting system, because children detected these errors for set sizes far greater than those they could accurately count themselves. Of course, although children could not verify the puppet's counts by counting the large sets themselves, they could count small sets. Thus, they may have learned the principles from exposure to the conventional counting system.

In fact, proponents of the principles-after view make just that argument—that children abstract the principles through experience with the counting routine (Briars & Siegler, 1984; Fuson, 1988). Several studies provide evidence for this position. Fuson (1988) found that early adherence to the counting principles breaks down for more challenging tasks, such as counting large or randomly arranged sets. And, in contrast to Gelman and Meck's (1983) results, Briars and Siegler found an age effect for detecting counting principle violations, such that 3-year-olds were less likely to object to one-to-one and stable order errors than were 4- and 5-year-olds. This finding suggests that an understanding of these principles develops as children acquire the count words. Furthemore, children's own counting is more accurate than their error detection, indicating the reverse of the order of acquisition reported by Gelman and Meck (Briars & Siegler, 1984; Frye, et al., 1989). Finally, Fuson, Pergamont, Lyons, and Hall (1985) found that children respond correctly to the question "how many" without understanding cardinality. Like Gelman and Gallistel (1978), they observed that when youngsters were asked how many objects were in a set, some correctly responded with the last word in the count. However, when Fuson et al. asked these children to identify the referent for that number word, the children pointed to the last object counted rather than to the whole set of objects. Only older children indicated that the last number word referred to the whole set. Thus, knowledge of the cardinality principle appeared to develop after conventional counting skills were well established.

Further support for the principles-after view comes from the finding that children may not start with fully generalizable counting routines. For example, preschoolers are less accurate when asked to count nonobjects, such as sounds, events, parts, and classes, than they are when counting physical objects (Schaeffer et al., 1974; Shipley & Shepperson, 1990; Wynn, 1990). In fact, children first learning to count sometimes refuse to count nonobjects, even though they readily count sets of objects (Wynn, 1990). These findings suggest that children do not realize that verbal counting can apply to any set of discrete entities (the abstraction principle) until they have already mastered the process of counting objects.

Although the question of whether principles precede or follow learning to count has played a central role in the counting literature, it may be a dead end. In its most extreme form (i.e., principled knowledge is either entirely present or entirely absent prior to conventional counting), this question may be impossible to test empirically because there is no distinct threshold between having no knowledge of the conventional counting system and mastery of it. By the time children can perform conventional counting tests like those we have described, they have already had years of exposure to conventional counting. So, even if they cannot perform accurate counts themselves, their ability to follow some procedures and detect errors may still be due to their limited exposure to conventional counting. At the same time, such tasks do not directly test the claim that children have access to a nonverbal counting procedure. Theoretically, children could quantify sets in accordance with the counting principles even before they have been exposed to conventional counting, but this possibility cannot be assessed using conventional counting tasks.

Some have rejected the extreme version of this debate as too simplistic, arguing instead for a bi-directional influence of informal knowledge and conventional skills from the start (Baroody, 1992; Baroody & Ginsburg, 1986; Fuson, 1988; Miller, 1992; Rittle-Johnson & Siegler, 1998). However, the idea of innate principles is all but lost in these models. For example, Baroody proposed an iterative or "mutual-development" model in which conceptual understanding and procedural skill build on each other in small increments. In this view, children might have a partial understanding of the counting principles that helps them carry out counting procedures. Gains in procedural skill would advance understanding of the counting principles. These advances would support further gains in counting skill, and so forth. At the least, this conceptualization assigns a much weaker role to innate knowledge than the principles-before view. In fact, the iterative model could hold true no matter what quantitative awareness infants possess. The claim is simply that children enter each learning episode with some conceptual understanding, but the earliest forms of this understanding could be inchoate, unorganized, and severely limited.

Does Nonverbal Quantification Help or Hinder Acquisition of Conventional Skills? In chapter 6, we discussed the proposal that children's nonverbal representations of quantity may promote learning in certain contexts but may *interfere* with learning in others. A strong proponent of this view is Gelman (1991; Gelman & Brenneman, 1994), who argues that using an accumulator helps children learn to count because the magnitudes it generates are analogous to the ordering of numbers on a number line. Therefore, learning to count verbally should be a fairly straightforward mapping of words onto preexisting cardinal representations. However, Gelman contends that learning about fractions should be quite difficult because the accumulator cannot represent quantities that fall between whole numbers.

As we discussed, in a weaker version of this conceptualization, Wynn (1995) agrees that the accumulator representation interferes with learning about fractions, but she also argues that the mapping between the accumulator and verbal counting is not straightforward. Thus, whereas the mapping between the accumulator magnitudes and the count words may be more transparent than for fraction names, it is nonetheless complex. Wynn's reasoning is that the magnitudes generated by the accumulator explicitly embody ordinal relations, whereas the count words derive ordinal meaning implicitly, based on their position in the count word list. Therefore, children would need to resolve these differences before they could integrate preverbal and verbal quantification. Wynn's position is supported by evidence of an 18-month lag between the time children first start to count around age 2 years and when they understand how counting determines cardinality (Wynn, 1990, 1992). During this lag, she argues, children are working to resolve the differences between their preverbal representations and the conventional counting system.

Other views of this mapping do not specify that the preverbal representation is either particularly helpful or particularly limiting. During the 1970s and 1980s, several investigators interpreted children's labeling of small sets as evidence that they were recognizing patterns via subitizing (Fuson, 1988; Schaeffer et al., 1974). Learning to count in this view involved learning the count word sequence and mapping individual words onto specific patterns. Supposedly the coordination of these two accomplishments led to a complete understanding of the meaning of counting. In this view, the preverbal system makes a positive contribution but is limited to only part of what children need to learn about counting and the meaning of numbers.

In our review of models of nonverbal quantitative representation, we concluded that the extant evidence favors Huttenlocher et al.'s (1994) mental models account. Although the mapping of count words onto this representation was not discussed in that paper, we speculate that it might be similar to the subitizing explanation. That is, the mental model for a set would provide an entity that could be labeled. Because the symbols in a mental model are assigned one to one, such a representation might model the one-to-one principle as well. The same would hold true for other object tokens accounts (e.g., Simon, 1997; Uller et al., 1999), the main difference being that these authors claim this one-to-one representation is available in infancy, whereas Huttenlocher et al. concluded that it emerges in early childhood.

At present, these accounts of the interaction between preverbal and verbal quantification are speculative and have not been tested directly. The idea that infants and young children can quantify sets nonverbally is still new, and until more is known about these early abilities, bridging the gap to research on conventional skills will be difficult. One thing is certain, though: preverbal and conventional representations do meet at some point in development. Therefore, as more is learned, it will be critical to continue integrating research on verbal counting with research on preverbal number concepts for a coherent developmental story to emerge. Next, we turn to the acquisition of another class of conventional skills, those associated with calculation. How does learning to add and subtract conventionally map onto preexisting nonverbal procedures?

Calculation

Learning to Add and Subtract

Informal notions of addition and subtraction are evident early in development. Even 5-month-olds respond to transformations that change quantities; they seem to expect that when an amount is added to an existing amount, the total will increase (Feigenson & Spelke, 1998; Gao et al., 1998; Uller et al., 1999; Wynn, 1994). Preschool children exhibit a more precise calculation ability. They are able to produce the exact solutions to small numerosity addition and subtraction problems using object sets by 3 years of age (Huttenlocher et al., 1994). Children do not solve analogous verbal problems without concrete supports until 5½ years of age (Levine et al., 1992).

What is happening while children make the transition from nonverbal to verbal calculation between 3 and 5 years of age? Undoubtedly, one accomplishment is learning the meaning of the count words. Before children can respond to either number fact problems (e.g., "What is two plus three?") or story problems (e.g., "John has two apples and then he gets three more. How many apples does John have?"), they must be able to interpret words like "two" and "three." As discussed before, we know that children learn the meanings of the words for small sets at about 2½ to 3 years of age. Soon after, at about 3½ years of age, they learn that the last word in a count stands for the cardinality of the counted set. This involves going from a counted set to a cardinal value. However, it may be some time before children can rapidly interpret the meanings of larger count words. To do so, they must reverse this process and go from a cardinal value to the hypothetical set it represents. Children must carry out this type of operation to interpret correctly the verbal symbols in a conventional problem.[1]

The Role of Concrete Referents

Concrete referents seem to be an important support for children making the transition from nonverbal to verbal calculation, perhaps because such referents can represent the aspects of verbal problems outlined before (i.e., cardinal value and discreteness). Children first succeed at solving conventional addition and subtraction problems when they use referents, such as fingers or blocks. For example, Carpenter and Moser

---

1. We refer here and throughout to problems presented orally rather than written. Although many of our conclusions might apply to performance on written problems as well, such problems involve another level of symbolic interpretation that has not been studied extensively in preschool children.

(1982) found that preschool children performed much better on calculation problems when blocks were provided than they did on problems without blocks. This difference between conditions persisted longer for problems involving larger numbers. Hughes (1981, 1986) has found that 3- to 5-year-old children solve conventional calculation problems with concrete supports best, followed by those in which they were asked to imagine the presence of those supports, and worst on those in which they were just given verbal number fact problems, (e.g., "What does one and two make?"). In fact, few children in this age range could solve the purely verbal problems. Similarly, Levine et al. (1992) found that children from 4 to 5 years of age were better at solving word problems that referred to objects than they were for number fact problems that made no reference to objects. As in Hughes's research, the youngest children performed near floor on the verbal number fact problems.

Clearly, concrete referents play a key role in the transition from nonverbal to conventional calculation. The question is what specific need these referents fill. Given the new demands that arise as children learn to calculate verbally, we suspect that concrete referents mainly remind children of the meanings of the count words. For example, when children encounter the problem $7 - 4$, they must translate the numeral 7 into its cardinal meaning: seven things. They must remind themselves what a set of seven individual things is. Although children might mentally represent small sets exactly, they likely cannot do so for larger numbers such as this, using only the preverbal representation. By laying out a set of objects to stand for the set, children are more likely to reach an accurate solution.

However, acting out calculation problems using concrete supports is cumbersome and time consuming. With development, perhaps as children become more proficient at interpreting numerals, they begin to discover calculation shortcuts. Consider the development of conventional addition. Adults can simply retrieve the answers to simple problems, such as $3 + 5$, from memory. However, children's memory for the number facts is initially limited or nonexistent. Therefore, 4- and 5-year-olds prefer to make a set of referents for each term and count the entire set. For example, to solve the problem $3 + 5$, they may hold up three fingers on one hand and five on the other and then count all the fingers. Children soon discover that they can get by with representing one addend with referents and simply counting up the other. Thus, for $3 + 5$, they could count 1-2-3 and then continue the count as they tagged each of five fingers (Baroody, Tiilikainen, & Liao, in press). By first grade, children have added a version of the *min* strategy to their repertoire (Ashcraft, 1982; Groen & Parkman, 1972; Siegler, 1987). In this strategy, children count the items in the smaller set starting with the cardinal value of the larger set. So, to solve the problem $5 + 3$, a child might hold up three fingers and count them "6, 7, 8." The min strategy is a useful shortcut; it is much faster and more accurate than counting all the items in both sets or starting with the smaller set and counting up from there (Siegler, 1987).

These are merely a few highlights of the strategies children generate as they are learning to add (see Baroody et al., in press, for a more detailed discussion). We point out here that this progression represents a move toward using the counting sequence to embody the cardinal value of a count word rather than using concrete referents. Eventually, children's recall of the number facts improves to the point that retrieval becomes the favored addition strategy (Ashcraft, 1982). In principle, the use of number facts does not require a representation of quantity at all because it is possible for someone to learn the facts as simple associations. However, in practice, children need to develop a sense of ordinality to detect retrieval errors (e.g., 3 + 1 = 2) and to prepare for more complicated forms of addition and subtraction (e.g., problems involving negative integers). The mastery of number facts, along with notions of decomposition, therefore seems to involve a final move away from concrete referents toward an internalized representation of the counting sequence. Children who do not develop this sense of ordinality may experience difficulty as more complex problems are encountered.

There are interesting educational implications of the notion that children use concrete referents to interpret the count words. Teachers are encouraged to introduce new math concepts to children via experiences with concrete models or "manipulatives." For example, a first grade teacher might introduce addition by presenting a simple problem using blocks to represent the amounts and moving them together to represent the addition transformation. Then children would be encouraged to practice by solving a series of similar addition problems using blocks for concrete support. Research on early quantitative development tells us that, although this practice is undoubtedly helpful for children, it may not be helpful for the reason that some educators think. The block activities are probably not necessary to convey the idea of quantitative transformation to children or to teach them how to solve such problems. Children already understand addition and subtraction by the time they enter school. Instead, the referents may simply be a sort of crib sheet for the meanings of the count words that children use until they have either internalized the words' ordinal meanings, memorized the number facts, or both. If so, this case highlights the importance of another educational tool for teaching calculation: the number line. In this approach, children are taught to move their fingers along a written number line to solve problems. For example, to solve 7 + 4, children would start with their fingers on 7 and then count to 4 as they moved their fingers one space for each word. Their fingers should stop on the correct solution, 11. Although children may

not immediately comprehend the number line without direct instruction (Van de Walle, 1994), once they have learned how to use it, it may
be a valuable tool for helping them internalize the ordinal meanings of
the number words and abandon their need for concrete supports. Of
course, this does not mean that concrete referents should be eliminated
from calculation instruction. Adding and subtracting with concrete referents can impart knowledge about the decomposition of numbers that
is crucial for the development of numeracy concepts and acquisition of
later mathematical skills (Nunes & Bryant, 1996). Calculation practice
with blocks may help children acquire these concepts, even if it does
not convey calculation concepts per se.

In summary, children already have a basic understanding of quantitative transformations by the time they are introduced to conventional
calculation in school. Yet it takes some time before children can solve
verbal number fact and word problems. This may reflect, in part, the
amount of time it takes to memorize the number facts. However, to
avoid retrieval errors and understand decomposition, children must do
more than solve calculation problems by rote memorization. They also
must be able to mentally represent the problem situations described by
the written or verbal symbols. Thus, another reason for the lag between nonverbal and verbal calculation skill might be that children are
learning to interpret the conventional symbols for numbers without
concrete support.

Measurement

The ability to obtain accurate representations of continuous quantity is
aided by the use of conventional units, such as inches, tablespoons, and
liters. As we argued in chapter 6, the most accurate way to estimate
amounts nonverbally is probably to compare one amount to another or
to an informal unit, as in "half a glass of water." Conventional measurement may provide the first opportunity for children to represent
amounts with any precision. As children acquire measurement concepts, there may be little in their preverbal repertoire to draw on. Instead, likely these concepts are built on a foundation of conventional
counting and the rote use of measurement tools. We next consider why
this is the case and how this development unfolds.

Counting and Measurement

Counting and measuring are closely related. In fact, counting is really
just a special type of measurement. In both cases the goal is to specify a
quantity in terms of a conventional representation. To do so, the quantity must be divided into units and the units totaled. In both counting

and measurement, the units are chosen in advance. Someone counting the number of tomatoes grown this summer would be using the whole tomato as the unit. Alternatively, the total tomato quantity could be measured by counting the number of pounds, bushels, cups or other conventional units. The main difference between counting and these other kinds of measurement is that, in counting, the units are given— the total is already divided into discrete items. In the other cases, the total must be divided by imposing some other unit.

Because conventional measurement requires counting and more, it is not surprising that conventional counting skills are acquired first. Measurement has the added demand of explicitly applying units to divide a total, which requires an explicit understanding of the nature of units and takes some time to develop. For example, children must learn that measurement units need to maintain a constant size. An inch is not an inch unless it is the exact same size as any other inch.[2] This allows us to infer that a "6-inch" submarine sandwich is half as long as a "12-inch" sandwich.

Several studies have shown that children fail to appreciate the importance of equal-sized units until quite late in development. Pettito (1990) asked elementary school children to decide which of several rulers they would like to use to measure a line. The rulers were marked with either standard units or units that varied greatly in size. The majority of first or second graders were content to use a ruler with variable units. Only about half of the third graders chose the standard ruler. This shows that most children lack a fundamental notion of unit until well into elementary school.

Consistent with this finding, Nunes and Bryant (1996) described the results of several studies showing that children are unaware that measurement units must have equal size. In one study, Nunes and colleagues gave 5- and 6-year-olds paper rulers with the units marked and asked them to write in the numbers. Rather than spacing the numbers equally, children tended to write them in haphazardly with no regard for the size of the spaces. Also, few children used zero as a starting point. This indicates that they fail to recognize that "1" on a ruler refers to the first unit. In another study, 5- to 7-year-olds were asked to decide which of two ribbons was longer, given a set of measurements. For example, children were told that one ribbon was 7 centimeters long and the other was 6 centimeters long. Children in all age groups had little difficulty judging which was longer in problems such as this where the units were the same. However, when the units were varied across ribbons, performance was much worse. For example, when children were told one ribbon was 2 inches long and the other was 2 centime-

---

2. At least to the extent possible, given that all measurements have some margin of error (Baroody, 1998).

ters, 5-year-olds performed at chance. Seven-year-olds performed better than chance but still did much worse than they had when the units were the same, even though all children in the study were familiar with both inches and centimeters and knew that inches were larger. They simply did not take unit size into account when comparing two measurements. Incidentally, this conceptual limitation is not observed only in measurement situations. Children make similar errors on conventional fraction problems. For example, when shown a circle divided into three unequal parts, such as one-half and two quarters, children nonetheless claim that each part is one-third of the circle (Baroody, 1987; Behr, Lesh, Post, & Silver, 1983).

The fact that children have difficulty recognizing the size equivalence of measurement units is puzzling because children need to understand equivalence classes in order to count. For example, counting all the red things in a pile of toys is essentially applying number to the equivalence class "red." It requires specifying that each of the units be equal in color. This is conceptually similar to deciding to count all items of an equal size, such as measurement units. Of course, counting red things does not involve accruing total redness in the same way that counting measurement units involves accruing total amount (e.g., total length is summed over equal units of length). Still, the idea of establishing equivalence for the sake of counting should help children see the equivalence of measurement units more readily than it apparently does.

Perhaps experience with equivalence classes in counting actually interferes more than it helps. As children learn to count, they learn that each individual counts the same as another, whether it is huge or tiny (unless, of course your goal is to count all items of a certain size). Thus, if your goal is to count animals, an elephant and a mouse are equal in number to two mice, even though the animals in the first set are very different from one another in size and the overall amount of animal differs greatly between the two sets. This idea may be quite salient to children, especially if they had previously been accustomed to estimating quantity based on overall amount. They may be so aware that size is irrelevant in conventional counting that they have trouble attending to size when they apply counting to measurement.

Another contributor to children's difficulty with equal-size units may be the overall complexity of the measurement act (e.g., Baroody, 1998). That is, children may be so overwhelmed with the basic act of measuring—choosing an appropriate measurement tool, using it correctly, and so forth—that they have few cognitive resources left to attend to unit size. Certain educational practices also encourage mechanical application of measurement tools without understanding. Traditional approaches that emphasize memorizing conversions (e.g., 12 inches equal one foot) and rote use of measurement tools do little to impart the idea of equal units and might leave children with a false impression of what measurement entails (Baroody, 1998).

Let's return to the larger issue of how the acquisition of measurement conventions relates to nonverbal quantification and counting. First, there is probably no direct mapping of conventional measurement onto nonverbal quantitative representation. Instead, measurement likely is built on conventional counting skills. Children do not exhibit any understanding of conventional measurement until 7 or 8 years of age, nearly 5 years after a nonverbal representation of discrete number has emerged. Although it might take even longer to grasp measurement without this preverbal foundation, the amount of lag suggests that more is happening during this period than a simple mapping.

Another reason to think that conventional counting serves as an intermediary between nonverbal quantitative representation and measurement is that the measurement act involves conventional counting. Even if children only read the numeral off a ruler without understanding what they are doing, they must know the count words. Furthermore, a real understanding of conventional measurement requires an awareness that measurement tools provide a shortcut for counting individual measurement units. Consistent with this interpretation, we know that counting system acquisition occurs midway between measurement and the nonverbal period. In fact, children can count for several years before they understand measurement. Perhaps mastery of the conventional counting system not only gives children a component skill for measurement but also lays some of the conceptual groundwork by introducing the idea that quantities can be represented using conventional units.

The fact that conventional measurement is acquired late relative to discrete number representation may also contribute to the conceptual differentiation of continuous and discrete quantification. Recall that in chapter 5 we proposed that infants and children start out using estimates of continuous amount to deal with quantitative problems. We argued that these estimates could serve a child well in many tasks but that eventually a precise representation would be desirable. There is evidence that children gain this precision around $2\frac{1}{2}$ to 3 years of age by using a mental model for small discrete sets (Huttenlocher et al., 1994). Certainly, the latest children would begin to represent exact number is around age $3\frac{1}{2}$ years, when they learn to count verbally. Either way, these discrete number processes would be available to children well before they can measure continuous amounts. Because children gain precision for discrete sets first, they should (and do) prefer to enumerate sets in terms of number when they can; however, they also rely on estimates of continuous amount as a default (e.g., when the set is too large to count). With development, children learn to measure continuous amounts by applying arbitrary conventional units. This would cement the idea that continuous and discrete quantities are distinct because measuring them requires different procedures. Thus, the time course by which children come to represent different kinds of quantity with precision may itself facilitate the realization that different kinds of quantity exist.

Children's Use of Measurement Tools

Although a real understanding of measurement units eludes children for some time, they are capable of using conventional measurement tools in a largely rote way. For example, Nunes, Light, and Mason (1993) found that 6- to 8-year-olds performed near ceiling when asked to compare two lengths using a standard ruler. However, this finding merely demonstrates that children can position the ruler correctly and then read the appropriate numbers. It does not indicate an understanding of unit measures. In fact, when Nunes et al. gave the same children a ruler that was altered so that simply reading the number led to an incorrect measure, 6-year-olds performed at chance.

It isn't too surprising that children would use measurement tools by rote at first. Such tools not only embody the idea of equal units but also the idea of unit hierarchies. For example, a standard ruler is marked off in inches, probably the unit used most commonly. However, rulers are often subdivided further into fractions of an inch. A whole ruler is also a unit in its own right. These hierarchies require notions of classification and decomposition akin to those involved in place value. These ideas are more complex in the case of imperial measurement, a system that does not adhere to a consistent base structure like the metric system. It would be reasonable to expect children to take some time to understand these hierarchies, but they may be able to use rulers by rote in the meantime, especially since traditional instruction tends to encourage rote use of measurement tools while failing to provide the experiences children need to make sense of these complicated relations (Baroody, 1998).

Finally, this pattern of using conventions in a rote manner before understanding seems to be the rule across conventions. Rather than acquiring conventional skills in a logical progression that builds neatly on prior knowledge, children seem to make as much progress as they can on multiple fronts. Eventually these pathways converge, and greater conceptual understanding arises. For example, children count by rote for some time before they understand the cardinal meaning of the count words. In the meantime, they also learn to label and match small sets. When these skills converge, children begin to make sense of the count words.

Just as for counting, the rote application of measurement procedures early in the learning process may contribute to conceptual understanding in the long run (though clearly this experience alone would not be sufficient). At the least, it introduces children to the conventional units used in their culture. It may also alert children to the various dimensions that can be measured (e.g., length, weight, height, etc.) and convey the idea of assigning a numerical value to these dimensions. It gives children practice carrying out the physical processes of measurement so that these become automatic. Of course, children need to integrate these specifics with broader concepts, such as equal units, unit hierarchies, and transitive inference, to fully grasp measurement procedures.

A particularly powerful insight might arise from the convergence of applying measurement tools by rote and measuring with single units. Rote measurement provides a number that stands for the value, along some dimension, of the thing to be measured (e.g., the length of a pencil is 8 inches), rather like the representation of the last word in a rote count, that is, the cardinality principle (Gelman & Gallistel, 1978). However, unlike counting, for which the individual units are highlighted, measurement tools obscure the individual units. Children might need the opportunity to count single units and see that the total is equal to the measurement obtained with a larger tool. For example, children might benefit from measuring the length of their favorite book once with 1-inch cards and again with a standard 12-inch ruler.

In summary, conventional measurement is difficult and takes children years to understand. There is probably no direct link between conventional measurement and children's preverbal representations. Instead, measurement is likely built through conventional counting practice and the rote use of other measurement tools. Because measurement follows learning to count, acquisition of this convention may reinforce the conceptual differentiation between discrete and continuous quantities. As such, this could be a case of conventions acting as a conceptual catalyst.

Fractions

One of the most well-known obstacles for American schoolchildren is mastering conventional fractions (e.g., Behr, Wachsmuth, Post, & Lesh, 1984). Children make many more errors on fraction problems than they do on whole number problems. Their errors often reflect a failure to grasp basic properties of fractions, such as the inverse relation between the number of fractional parts and the size of these parts. For example, children frequently add numerators and denominators together with apparent disregard for the part-whole relations these symbols are intended to represent (e.g., $3/4 + 1/2 = 4/6$) (Resnick & Ford, 1981). Even when children solve fraction problems accurately, they often do not appear to understand the reasoning behind the symbol manipulations (Kerslake, 1986). For example, 12- to 14-year-olds who correctly solved problems like $\frac{3}{4} + \frac{1}{2}$ by finding a common denominator could not explain why they did so. Instead, they seemed to apply by rote the procedure they had been taught in school without understanding the motivation for doing it.

As discussed in detail in chapter 6, the length of time it takes children to master conventional fractions and the kinds of errors they make have led some to conclude that the difficulty is rooted in the structure of innate numerical representations (Gelman, 1991; Wynn, 1997). This representation, they contend, is ideally suited for extracting and representing whole number information but cannot accommodate quantities that fall between whole units. However, we know that when young children are tested without the use of conventional symbols, they can compare, order, and calculate with fractions. These skills are evident years before children learn how to solve such problems using conventional symbols. Thus, it seems unlikely that children's difficulties in learning fraction conventions are due to an innate limitation.

In the following sections, we consider how conventional fraction skills map onto children's earlier informal knowledge of relative quantity. We also discuss possible sources of difficulty that might explain why conventional fractions are so hard for children to understand, even after acquiring some of the necessary underlying concepts.

The Mapping between Fraction Symbols and Nonverbal Representation

Children first begin to deal with conventional fractions by learning the symbols for them, mapping between conventional fraction names (e.g., $\frac{1}{2}$ and one half) and their conceptual referents. Children do not likely think about fractional quantities in a way that corresponds neatly to the verbal system, so this mapping is probably not straightforward. For example, a child who sees a glass of milk three-quarters full may have an approximate sense of the proportion of milk in the glass. However, he is unlikely to have mentally divided the glass into four equal parts and estimated that only three of these parts contain milk. To do so would require measuring the milk into equal units—a skill that emerges relatively late and builds on other conventional abilities.

But what about discrete sets for which equal units are already imposed? One would assume that the conventional symbols for fractions would map more easily to these quantities. However, to see this mapping, children would need to understand something about hierarchies, subsets, and the additive composition of discrete numbers. As we know from Piaget's research, category hierarchies are not obvious to children. He found that children are unable to judge whether there are more items in a total set or a subset until 7 or 8 years of age. For example, when shown a set with ten daisies and five roses, children were unable to judge whether there were more daisies or more flowers. Word problems involving additive composition (i.e., the idea that a set of 8 is made up of 3 and 5, 2 and 6, etc.) are also quite difficult for children at 5 and 6 years of age (Nunes & Bryant, 1996). Even if children could overcome these conceptual challenges, they would also need a way to represent the exact number of items before they learn to count. Although they may use a mental model to represent small sets exactly, this would not help them understand fraction names such as ⅚. Thus, one way or another, the acquisition of fraction conventions likely depends on prior knowledge of other conventions, including counting and measurement.

Teachers certainly capitalize on conventional counting skills to introduce fraction symbols, often by demonstrating an approach called "double-counting" (Nunes & Bryant, 1996). In this approach, a whole, such as a pie, is shown divided into equal parts. Some of the parts are colored to indicate a fractional amount. Children are taught to count the number of colored parts to determine the numerator and the total number of pieces to determine the denominator. By fifth grade, the youngest age group tested, children are quite proficient at this strategy. However, double-counting may lead to conceptual difficulties later on. First, this approach promotes a narrow view of fractions that emphasizes part-whole relations. This thinking may hinder learning about other fractional relations, such as division or ratios. Second, double-counting encourages children to apply rote procedures to fraction tasks that do not require an understanding of equal units. This rote application of procedures would make it more difficult to solve problems that require attention to unit size (e.g., $\frac{3}{8} + \frac{3}{4}$). Finally, using counting in this way may increase children's tendency to confuse whole number and fraction symbols (as we discuss later).

Although double-counting is a prevalent means of teaching fraction notation, not all fraction names are learned this way. Hunting and Sharpley (1988) found that preschool children spontaneously acquire an approximate understanding of the term "one half." For one task, these investigators asked children to divide a clay sausage in half. A significant proportion of the children (35%) cut the sausage at about the midpoint, even though they did not measure it in any conventional or precise way. When asked to divide a deck of 12 cards in half, few children (11%) did so exactly; however, the majority of responses clustered around 6, which indicated that children had approximated the division. Thus, children seem to learn the term "one half" in an inexact sense before they are introduced to other fraction names.

Cumulatively, these findings suggest a possible scenario for the mapping between fraction notation and nonverbal representations of quantity. If infants start out approximating quantities based on relative amount, they might have a sense of part-part or part-whole relations, but they would not represent quantity in equal size units as we do with fraction symbols (e.g., $^3/_8$ means 3 of 8 equal size parts). Thus, whereas such a representation might lay some of the conceptual groundwork for fractions and proportions, it would provide nothing that the fraction symbols could map onto directly. Neither would the mental model for small discrete sets that we have argued emerges in preschool, because this representation, like counting, does not depend on equal-size units. Furthermore, it does not involve relating quantities to each other or to whole units. Thus, there is no reason to expect the mental model to help the child learn conventional fraction symbols. Children may be able to interpret the fraction term "one half" because one half embodies the simplest quantitative relation—one part equal to another—that can be determined using comparisons of overall amount. However, children must wait until they acquire conventional counting skills to interpret other fraction names accurately via double counting. Eventually, children would need to understand equal units to fully comprehend the meaning of fraction symbols.

Why Are Conventional Fractions Difficult?

We have proposed that infants and young children have informal notions of relative quantity. Indeed, we have claimed that in this basic way all quantities are represented at first. If so, why are conventional fractions so hard to learn? We have already identified one reason: children must learn to count and understand equal units to grasp fraction notation. Another reason is that they may confuse the symbols for whole numbers with those for fractions (Hunting, 1986; Hunting & Sharpley, 1988; Mack, 1993; Mix et al., 1999). Children learning the fraction symbols do not start with a blank slate where mathematical conventions are concerned—they already know about the symbols for whole numbers (i.e., the counting system). Indeed, these symbols play a key role in instruction on fraction notation, especially when children are taught double-counting to interpret fraction names. This prior knowledge of whole number conventions could cause interference because the numerals used to represent fractions mean something different from the same numerals used to represent whole numbers (Baroody, 1998). For example, 4 is greater than 3 but $^1/_4$ is less than $^1/_3$. Under these circumstances, it isn't surprising that children would make errors that reflect a whole number bias.

The same kind of interference is possible as children learn the procedures for manipulating fraction symbols. Specifically, the digits used in fraction problems may call to mind whole number procedures already familiar to children (Baroody, 1998). Recall that a common fraction addition error is to sum both the numerators and denominators (e.g., $^1/_2 + ^1/_4 = ^2/_6$). This is not simply a mindless error that shows children do not understand the nature of fractions. Instead, it reflects the inappropriate application of a procedure that works in whole number situations. This is not to say that finding a common denominator and then adding wouldn't be more complicated than whole number addition even if there were no interference. However, because children must suppress whole number concepts when they encounter fraction symbols, the difficulty probably increases.

The influence of whole number concepts also appears in children's strategies for solving fraction problems. For example, a predominant early strategy is the use of partitioning (Mack, 1993). Consider a story problem in which a student is asked to figure out how much pizza is left if someone has eaten $4/6$. To solve this problem by partitioning, the student would mentally or physically divide a pizza into six pieces, take out four, and then count up the remaining pieces. Children often use partitioning to solve conventional fraction problems. When nonconventional procedures are used, partitioning still seems to be the easiest problem type for children to solve (Correa, 1995; Sophian et al., 1997). The drawback to partitioning is that, like double-counting, it promotes a narrow view of fractions. To partition, one needs only to see fractions as part-whole relations. Children who rely on the partitioning strategy may have more trouble comprehending other meanings of fractions, such as many-to-one relations that can be expressed in ratios (e.g., distributing two sheets of paper to every child in a classroom).

The preceding account can explain why children are confused by fraction conventions and make whole number errors. However, it does not explain why children's early knowledge of relative quantity remains disconnected from their use of fraction conventions. In other words, why don't the concepts evident in preschool turn out to be more helpful later on? How do children manipulate fraction symbols, whether incorrectly or correctly, for years without seeming to understand what they are doing or why? Again, the use of whole number conventions to deal with fraction conventions is a likely answer. It may not be possible to map fraction symbols onto children's preverbal representations in any meaningful way. Although the use of whole number conventions gives children a key to understanding fraction notation in the short term, it may drive a wedge between children's use of fraction conventions and their underlying informal concepts.

Unfortunately, the confusion between whole number and fraction concepts may be unavoidable. To fully understand what fractions represent, one needs an idea of equal units, counting, subsets, and so forth. In other words, fraction notation and whole number notation are confusable precisely because the underlying concepts are inextricably linked. In the process of overcoming this confusion, children can sort out some important relations. Therefore, a reasonable goal for educators might be to recognize this confusion for what it is and help children move beyond it rather than try to avoid it entirely from the outset.

Instructor: When you add fractions, how do you add them?

Tony: Across. Add the top numbers across and the bottom numbers across.

Instructor: I want you to think of the answer to this problem in your head. If you had 3/8 of a pizza and I gave you 2/8 more pizza, how much pizza would have?

Tony: Five-eighths. (Goes to his paper on his own initiative and writes 3/8+2/8 =, gasps, stops, then writes 5/8.) I don't think that's right. I don't know. I think this (the 8 in 5/8) just might be 16. I think this'd be 5/16.

Instructor: Let's use our pieces to figure this out. (Tony gets out 3/8 and 2/8 of the fraction circle and puts the pieces together.) Now how much do you have?

Tony: Five-eighths. It seems like it would be sixteenths . . . This is hard.

FIGURE 8.1 Sample protocol from Mack's (1993) instructional approach.

For example, teachers might be explicit about the fact that the digits are being used in a new way when they stand for fractional amounts.

Finally, what happens to the preexisting nonverbal concepts while this sorting is going on? These concepts may continue to develop on a separate trajectory and become the informal knowledge of fractions that we use even as adults. For example, if one wanted to follow a recipe for four people but alter it to make three servings, one could calculate the precise conversions for each ingredient. However, it might be faster to measure each ingredient and dump out about ¼ of it. This intuitive approach is part of children's repertoire when they are struggling with fraction notation in elementary and junior high school, but, without explicit instruction, they may not see that the two are connected. Mack (1990, 1993) juxtaposes abstract symbolic problems with everyday situations to promote this integration. (See figure 8.1.) Cognitive dissonance occurs as children see that their formal solutions are not physically plausible. By moving back and forth between the written problem and everyday situations, Mack leads children to resolve the conflict themselves and emerge with a better understanding of what the symbols and procedures represent.

In summary, fractions, like measurement, are learned slowly and with difficulty. Although children have preexisting concepts to draw upon, the mapping between these concepts and fraction notation is not direct. Therefore, children learn fraction conventions using their knowledge of whole number conventions instead. This usage is problematic, though, because the same symbols are used differently in these two contexts. This variation can cause children to make whole number errors when dealing with fractions. It also leads children to develop their knowledge of fraction symbols separately from the underlying concepts the symbols are meant to represent. Eventually, this confusion can be resolved if children are encouraged to reconnect the conventions they have learned to their informal knowledge.

Conclusions

By the time children are introduced to conventional symbols, they already have an informal sense of many basic concepts based on preverbal quantification. Still, acquiring conventional symbols is not always straightforward because of differences between the preverbal and verbal systems. Counting and calculation may map more directly onto preverbal notions than either fractions and measurement. Children commonly use conventions in a rote manner for some time before they figure out what the conventions actually represent. Ideally, this rote use of the conventions converges with other ideas and experiences to form integrated concepts. Sometimes this merging cannot happen without formal instruction that makes these connections explicit. In all cases, learning the conventions can become a conceptual catalyst: it helps children transcend their preverbal concepts and attain new levels of understanding.

9

The Whole Child

Developmental psychologists commonly describe change within separate areas of cognition, as if each area developed independently of the others. Indeed, in this book we have focused exclusively on development in the quantitative domain. However, quantitative concepts do not emerge in isolation. At each opportunity to learn about quantity, a child brings along all of his learning—from language, categorization, and more (Thelen & Smith, 1994). Viewed this way, the development of any competence is less straightforward than it might at first seem. In this final chapter, we will attempt to address the complexity of these interarea influences. But first, we will briefly summarize our main conclusions about quantitative development.

Four Key Issues Revisited

What Changes from Infancy to Early Childhood?

Research on quantitative development has traditionally focused on either infancy or preschool age. From these different orientations, two distinct perspectives on development have emerged. On one hand, research with preschoolers has highlighted the mistakes and conceptual shortcomings of children in this age range. Some investigators have concluded that quantitative concepts are limited prior to acquisition of conventional skills. On the other hand, research with infants has highlighted the unexpected capabilities of young subjects. Based on this re-search, some investigators have concluded that humans are born with basic quantitative understandings wired in. In this latter view, subsequent changes are less significant—limited to making innate concepts explicit and integrating them with conventional symbols. One of the main aims of this book was to reexamine the course of quantitative development by synthesizing the research across these age groups. When we reviewed the infancy and preschool literatures with this transition in mind, a more moderate position emerged. That is, preschoolers have developed some notions about quantity, but these do not seem to spring directly from innate knowledge structures.

Several foundational skills are evident in infancy. One of the most robust is the ability to discriminate small sets. This ability has been shown for a variety of set types, including visual displays and sequential actions (Antell & Keating, 1981; Canfield & Smith, 1996; Starkey & Cooper, 1980; Starkey et al., 1990; Strauss & Curtis, 1981; Wynn, 1996). Infants also seem to anticipate the results of quantitative transformations (Gao et al., in press; Simon et al., 1996; Wynn, 1994). These findings demonstrate that infants can process quantitative information and detect important properties such as invariance and transformation. This starting point is richer than that hypothesized in previous developmental accounts, such as Piaget's.

Still, the presence of these early skills is not the whole story. Our review revealed substantial changes occurring after infancy but prior to acquisition of the conventional counting system. One change was in the ability to represent the exact number of individuals in a set. Not only do the published studies fail to prove that infants can represent precise numbers of items, but recent research indicates that infants use overall amount instead of number to perform quantitative tasks (Clearfield & Mix, 1999; Feigenson & Spelke, 1998). This indicates that there is a fundamental change in childhood from representations based on overall amount, which are inherently inexact, to representations based on exact number. This shift might occur between 2½ and 3 years of age, before which children give approximate responses (Huttenlocher et al., 1994). That is, when given a problem where the solution is three, young 2-year-olds are likely to produce two, three, or four items, but not wildly incorrect responses, such as nine. Around their third birthdays, children began to generate exact responses—they reliably produced exact matches for sets up to two items and some solved calculation problems correctly up to a total set size of two. We believe this shift could reflect a change in the underlying representation. Two possibilities are consistent with the current data. One is that the approximate responses of young 2-year-olds were based on continuous amount, as in infancy, and that children continue to use overall amount until they begin to represent exact discrete number around age 3 years. Another possibility is that there is an intermediate stage during which children use an inexact representation of discrete number before the exact representation emerges. The approximate responses of 2-year-olds could reflect the use of such an inexact but number-based representation.

Another significant change during early childhood is in the range of set sizes that can be processed. Specifically, infants respond to tasks involving only one to three items. Young children also exhibit set size limits but across a wider range (up to four or five items). Thus, set size limits are present across the age range, but the range increases somewhat with age. All models of preverbal representation can explain the set size limits in infancy, but none alone can account for the small increase observed in early childhood. For example, some have claimed that the magnitude representations generated by the accumulator become more variable as the true numerosity increases (i.e., scalar variability). Thus, representations of 20 would be more variable than representations of 10. This might explain why infants can discriminate 2 from 3 but not 4 from 5. However, it does not explain why young children can perform tasks with four or more items, even though the effects of scalar variability should be constant across the preverbal age range.

We propose that this shift reflects a change in representation. If infants are using overall amount to represent quantity, they should start out limited to small sets because these have the greatest proportional difference in amount, assuming that the items are the same size. Once children begin using a one-to-one process to represent discrete number, they could extend to larger sets because the proportional amount of stuff is no longer relevant. However, this would not mean that children could represent any number of items. They might be limited to sets less than six if they do not know the meanings of larger count words. A mental models representation would also be limited by the number of slots or tokens that can be maintained in memory simultaneously.

A final change is that children gradually abstract quantity across a wider range of contexts during the preschool period. Children's earliest recognition of equivalence between sets depends on the surface features of the items. Specifically, children can make identity matches before they recognize equivalence across more disparate items (Mix, 1999b). Over several months, children gradually extend to comparisons between different objects, such as lion figurines and black dots. Eventually, they can recognize equivalence between heterogeneous object sets or sets of events. This pattern parallels the changes observed in children's comparisons more generally: children start out making literal similarity matches and gradually extend to comparisons with fewer shared surface features until they can detect purely relational matches (for a discussion, see Gentner et al., 1995; and Smith, 1989).

How Does Continuous Quantity Fit In?

The second key issue we addressed was whether sensitivity to continuous amount emerges in infancy and how developing conceptualizations of continuous and discrete quantity are related. Recent studies indicate not only that infants use continuous amount to perform quantitative tasks (Gao et al., 2000; Newcombe et al., 1999) but also that they fail to respond to number when amount is equated (Clearfield & Mix, 1999; Feigenson & Spelke, 1998). Thus, continuous amount plays a much larger role in quantitative development than previously believed. In short, it may be the basic way infants view quantitative situations.

We speculated that the particular representation used by infants is based on relative rather than absolute amount. For example, rather than estimating the sheer amount of juice in a glass, infants might estimate what part of the glass is filled with juice, either by using the glass as a unit or comparing the empty and full parts to each other. If it is natural for infants to view quantities in relational terms, then this pattern should be evident in young children as well. Indeed, rather than being unable to process relative quantities in childhood, as some have claimed (e.g., Gelman, 1991; Wynn, 1995), preschoolers can perform informal relative quantity tasks long before they master conventional symbols for fractions.

This conceptualization implies that continuous and discrete quantities are not separated in infancy. However, at some time between infancy and school age, children begin to differentiate the two. We proposed that children make this distinction through the use of procedures that apply only to discrete physical objects. We specifically highlighted the potential contribution of a mental model. That is, once children can represent sets of objects using a mental model, they may find that they can be more accurate than they are when using relative quantity estimates. However, the one-to-one process underlying a mental model would not apply to continuous amounts, so children would still be inexact when dealing with such quantities. By applying the mental model to different situations, children would begin to divide the world into quantities that can be represented exactly and those that cannot. This division corresponds roughly to the discrete/continuous distinction (with the possible exception of sequential sets; see Mix, 1999a). Also, the tokens used in a mental model need not preserve information about amount to represent number. Applying a mental model would provide an opportunity to see that individuation is sometimes more informative than overall amount—another clue that continuous and discrete quantities are different.

The same arguments could be made for other procedures that apply to discrete objects. For example, children might learn that discrete and continuous quantities are different because only discrete quantities can be shared fairly using a "one for you; one for me" strategy. Similarly, children might learn that amount can be ignored in favor of number by discovering that the same object name can apply to items that differ in size (e.g., a chihuahua and a mastiff are both called "dog"). We do not argue for the importance of one of these explanations over another but rather suggest a mechanism by which discrete and continuous quantities might be differentiated—through acquisition of any procedure that works differently for each quantity type. An interesting direction for future research might be to examine how acquiring one or a combination of these procedures contributes to this differentiation.

Acquisition of measurement conventions could solidify this conceptual distinction for children. For example, in measuring continuous amount, the size of the units is crucial. Cups are meaningful units only if one cup of sand is the same size as another cup of sand. In contrast, discrete physical objects can be used as units without being the same size (e.g., a set of three animals could include a duck, a whale, and a flea). Thus, as children learn to use conventional measurement tools, they receive additional information about how these quantities differ. Through applying unit measures, they learn that quantifying continuous amounts can never be precise. Even when one applies equal-sized units to continuous amounts, measurement error renders this quantification inexact. However, an exact count of discrete objects is possible regardless of differences (large or small) in the size of units.

How Is Quantity Represented before Children Learn to Count?

We asked which of several proposed models (subitizing, the accumulator, object representation, and mental models) best characterized the preverbal representation of quantity. We concluded that the mental models view provides the best account of findings in the existing literature.

Most notably, all except the mental models view assume that infants perceive quantity in terms of discrete number. The finding that infants use overall amount instead casts doubt on this assumption. In addition, each of the models has specific weaknesses. Item subitizing cannot explain how infants could represent quantitative transformations. Furthermore, whereas subitizing per se has been demonstrated in adults and school-age children, it has not been shown in preschool children or infants. The accumulator model cannot provide a parsimonious explanation of subtraction. It also predicts that sequential sets should be easier to enumerate than static sets—a prediction that runs counter to the developmental evidence. Because object representation accounts hold that infants assign tokens in parallel, they cannot explain performance on sequential tasks. Also, these accounts are inconsistent with the shift from approximate to exact representation evident in preschool (Huttenlocher et al., 1994) and the gradual decontextualization of numerical equivalence judgments (Mix, 1999b; Mix et al., 1996).

Taken together, the evidence suggests that there are two nonverbal representations of quantity: one that emerges in infancy and is based on relative amount and a second that emerges in early childhood and is based on discrete number. But what processes underlie these two representations? Currently no model can explain how infants represent overall amount. To develop such a model, additional research should specify which aspects of a visual scene infants use to determine quantity. For example, Clearfield and Mix (1999) explicitly varied overall amount in terms of contour length but allowed area and brightness to covary with contour length. To understand how infants process quantitative information, one needs to know whether they use contour length exclusively, contour length combined with area or brightness, or one of the other variables independent of contour length. Moreover, the hypothesis that infants use relative amount rather than absolute amount, though theoretically compelling, has yet to be tested directly. Ultimately, we need a bridge between the data on quantitative development and the facts of visual perception and representation at a neural level.

Regarding the second representation, there is evidence that the process for representing discrete number develops around the same age as other forms of symbolic thought, such as language, model use, and pretend play (Huttenlocher et al., 1994). Thus, it might be a number-specific byproduct of more general developmental changes. In chapter 7, we explored the possibility that children's mental models for number take object representations as input. That is, the symbols that stand for each item in a set could start out as object files or FINSTs. In contrast to current object representation accounts, we did not posit that *infants* use these spatial pointers to represent number. Instead, we proposed that infants use the pointers to differentiate objects and only later, in the preschool years, would children start to apply them to quantitative situations. Also during this period, children would become increasingly proficient at tailoring their object representations to particular tasks by learning to identify and eliminate extraneous details.

From an adaptive point of view, the proposed mental models representation may seem superfluous since children usually learn to count verbally soon after it appears. However, a mental model might play two critical roles at this time. As we argued, the advent of mental models might jumpstart the process of differentiating children's concepts of discrete and continuous quantity. A mental model might also act as a bridge to the acquisition of the conventional symbol system. For example, sets represented as mental models could be used as conceptual referents for the count words or to form equivalence classes.

*How Do Conventional Skills Map onto
the Nonverbal Representation?*

This leads to the fourth key issue considered in this book—namely, how nonverbal quantitative abilities interact with acquisition of conventional skills. We determined that this interaction takes several different forms. One, a direct mapping between conventional symbols and nonverbal representation, may occur only for acquisition of the counting system. In other cases, the mappings are more complex. For example, because conventional measurement requires an understanding of the count words, it involves the integration of familiar conventions (counting) with unfamiliar conventions (using a ruler) and nonverbal knowledge (experience dividing amounts into equal-size units).

Once children learn conventional symbols, they gain considerable conceptual power and flexibility. Not until children learn to count can they recognize equivalence in more abstract comparisons and represent the exact number of events (Mix, 1999a, 1999b). Acquiring conventional calculation skills allows children to solve more complex problems than they can solve nonverbally. The use of conventional symbols to represent continuous and relative amounts allows greater precision than the nonverbal representation. Consequently, learning to use conventional unit measures may further solidify children's concepts of continuous and discrete quantification. It certainly must lead to a better understanding of the relations among countables, masses, and units. More specifically, counting and measurement together act as a gateway that allows a bi-directional translation of continuous and discrete quantities. For example, measuring a pile of sand into cups translates a continuous amount into a discrete set of units. Conversely, if naturally occurring units are removed, as in pureeing a bunch of bananas, a discrete set can be transformed into a continuous amount, which can then be quantified relatively (e.g., half a bowlful) or discretely using conventional measurement units (e.g., 3 cups). When children learn to count and measure, they have the impetus to explore these relations.

Educators have been concerned that children apply conventions in a rote way that does not reflect understanding of the underlying mathematical concepts (e.g., Baroody, 1998). To address this problem, instructors teach mathematics with concrete materials to impart conceptual understanding. However, research with preschoolers has revealed that children have an informal understanding of many basic concepts before they enter school. Thus, these concrete supports probably serve more to help children bridge the gap between conventional symbols and their preexisting concepts. This suggests that educators should place greater emphasis on the connections between symbols and experiences rather than simply providing the experiences themselves (Baroody, 1998).

In considering these four key issues, we touched on the role of many skills beyond the quantitative domain, including language, categorization, and spatial cognition. In the sections that follow, we consider the connections to these other areas in more detail. Because the child brings all of his development to every learning situation, the actual processes by which children integrate these skills are much richer than the connections we can describe here. However, by identifying possible points of contact, we hope to suggest new lines of research that can begin to address this complexity.

Development across Areas

Categorization

It almost goes without saying that categorization is closely tied to quantitative concepts, just as it is closely tied to any other concept. Indeed, discussions of the relation between class and number have a long history, most notably in the work of Russell and Piaget. However, whereas these connections have been recognized in the philosophy of number, they are not often the focus of developmental research. In this section, we will highlight how the development of categorization might influence the development of quantitative concepts.

One aspect of the relation between quantification and categorization is that notions of quantity can apply only to that which has been categorized. In other words, before one counts, it is necessary to define what is to be counted—all the blue things on my desk, all the cows in the meadow, and so forth. This suggests that an understanding of quantity could not emerge prior to recognition of other categories. Of course, this point may be trivial given that many habituation studies have shown infants can discriminate between object categories (Cohen & Younger, 1983; Mandler & Bauer, 1993; Oakes, Madole, & Cohen, 1991; Ross, 1980). One might ask, however, whether these results demonstrate an awareness of equivalence classes or simply a response generalization that implies equivalence (i.e., Smith's [1993] explicit-implicit distinction). We have argued here and elsewhere that number habituation experiments can be explained in terms of response generalizations (Mix, 1999b). The same argument could apply to habituation to object categories. If so, then infants might not think about quantity as an amount of a particular category (e.g., three pieces of fruit or half a glass of juice) because establishing a category before quantifying it would require explicit grouping.

An alternative possibility is that infants do not relate quantity to other categories the way adults do. At the implicit level, these two notions may be distinct—that is, perceiving quantity may be perceiving quantity, regardless of what is in the set. It might reduce to something as simple as how much of the visual field is consumed by one area versus another. We cannot know for sure because number experimenters have eliminated the need to categorize by constraining infants' attention. Habituation experiments usually take place in a dim room in which the display is bright and salient, whereas all else is curtained off. Such an approach does not replicate the naturalistic situation in which an infant would have to select a set out of the environment before quantifying it. Even in preschool number experiments, such as our own matching tasks, children do not have to choose a category before estimating quantity—the categories are defined by what is on a standard card, what is in the experimenter's set, and so forth. This trend raises an interesting empirical question: when and how do children learn to coordinate number with other categories? At present, we do not know the answer, but more naturalistic studies that require categorization *and* quantification would provide a start. For example, infants could be habituated to a group of three dogs presented in a field of other animals. Would they respond to a novel number of dogs at test? Would it matter if the number of other animals shifted, too?

Another aspect of number's relation to categorization is that each number itself can be defined as a class or category that contains sets of a particular number of items (Russell, 1919/1993). For example, the category of two would include all groups of two, the category of three would include all groups of three, and so forth. When numbers are viewed as categories, then the research on children's comparisons has potentially important implications for quantitative development. Specifically, this research has identified several conditions that promote categorization and analogical transfer. If number categories are like other categories, then the same conditions also might promote number concept development.

Early comparisons depend on a high degree of similarity along many dimensions, not just those relevant to a particular task (DeLoache, 1989; Gentner & Rattermann, 1991; Holyoak, Junn, & Billman, 1984; Smith, 1989). Children are better able to retell stories accurately when the characters involved look the same and play the same roles (Gentner & Toupin, 1986). Likewise, children initially match items by color only when the items are identical or highly similar (e.g., red cars) and later extend to dissimilar items (e.g., red car and red crayon) (see Sandhofer & Smith, 1999, for a discussion). Shared surface features invite a comparison with the potential to reveal less obvious commonalities (Gentner & Rattermann, 1991; Smith, 1989). Over the course of development, mappings based on more abstract, specific, dimensions become possible. For instance, an experienced chess player would be able to see common patterns across chess boards that differed in the appearance of the pieces, size, and so forth. At the most abstract level, people can recognize relational similarity even in the case of cross-mapping, when surface features conflict with relations (e.g., seeing chess patterns as equivalent even when the roles of the particular pieces are interchanged).

If shared surface features promote category learning in general, could they also promote learning of numerical categories? Indeed, there is already reason to believe that such is the case. Recall that preschool children fail to recognize disparate sets as numerically equivalent. They first recognize equivalence only when both sets contain highly similar items (Mix, 1999b; Mix et al., 1996). This result might reflect the same focus on surface or overall similarity seen in other early comparisons. If so, attention to numerically irrelevant commonalities in two identical sets may be what leads children to notice the underlying relation of numerical equivalence and begin to abstract numerical categories. For example, when children see three cookies on one plate and three cookies on another, they may be drawn to make a comparison between the sets because the cookies look alike, the plates look alike, and so forth. In the process of making this comparison, children have the opportunity to notice that the number of cookies is also the same. In contrast, a child who sees three cookies on a plate and three flowers in a vase would have no reason to compare the two sets unless he already knew that number was a potential dimension of commonality.

Consistent with this interpretation is the finding that children are more likely to abstract a property that they have learned via literal comparisons (Klibanoff & Waxman, 2000; Kotovsky & Gentner, 1996). Kotovsky and Gentner used a triad matching task to test whether children could recognize relational similarity between sets of pictures. For example, children were shown a set of three circles that increased in size and had to match that set of circles to a set of three squares that also increased in size. This was a relatively literal comparison because the two sets shared similarity along the same dimension (i.e., size). In a more abstract version, the similarity was shared *across* dimensions. For example, children were asked to match three circles that increased in size with three circles that were the same size but increased in color saturation. By age 6 years, children reliably matched sets in both conditions. However, 4-year-olds exceeded chance on only the same-dimension comparisons: they performed randomly on the more abstract matches. This pattern echoes previous research showing that high similarity matches are easier for children to recognize initially. Of most interest here are the results of subsequent experiments aimed at helping 4-year-olds overcome their difficulty with cross-dimension matches. Specifically, when 4-year-olds were trained to criterion on same-dimension matches (e.g., size increase to size increase), they performed significantly above chance on the cross-dimension matches (e.g., size increase to color increase).

Klibanoff and Waxman (2000) reported similar findings in a word learning experiment. These investigators taught 3- and 4-year-olds novel words for patterns, such as *blickish* for "spotted". All the children were introduced to the property with the same item (e.g., "This is a *blickish* snake.") Then they were asked to indicate which of two items had the same property (e.g., "Which of these is *blickish*?"). The critical manipulation was that half of the children chose between items from the same basic level category as the training trial (e.g., a spotted snake and a plain snake), and the other half chose between members of a novel category (e.g., a spotted dog and a plain dog). Not surprisingly, children performed better when the choice was from within the same basic category—what was essentially an identity match. Most interesting, however, was that children tested this way went on to make more abstract matches. When children in both groups were given a second test trial that required extending the property across categories, the ones who had been tested on within-category exemplars performed significantly better. This finding suggests that children build abstract concepts from literal similarity matches.

Kotovsky and Gentner (1996) proposed that children learn to make abstract comparisons via high similarity matches through a process of progressive alignment. They reasoned that high similarity comparisons encourage and facilitate comparisons because the shared features highlight a variety of comparable dimensions or points of alignment. Consider a comparison between two cairn terriers. Both dogs would share a multitude of features: brown fur, stocky body, long tail, pointed ears, overall small stature, and so forth. Each of these commonalities highlights a point of alignment: color, build, tail length, and so forth. Kotovsky and Gentner argued that high similarity comparisons draw children into the aligning process so that they become aware of these possible dimensions and then will look for them in future comparisons. Thus, after comparing cairn terriers, a child would be more likely to look for body build similarity in two otherwise different dogs.

If progressive alignment underlies development of numerical comparisons, then two predictions follow. First, children should recognize equivalence for high similarity equivalence judgments before they can match sets with only number in common. This prediction has already been borne out. Specifically, children can match identical sets almost one year before they recognize numerical equivalence for sets that do not look alike (Huttenlocher, et al., 1994; Mix, 1999b; Mix et al., 1996). A second prediction is that children who have had experience matching identical sets would be more likely to recognize equivalence in abstract comparisons. Currently no empirical work directly tests this prediction. It is worth noting that in Mix's matching experiments, half the children received a block of literal similarity trials before the more disparate comparisons through counterbalancing. If experience with literal similarity trials promotes numerical abstraction, then one might expect significant order effects; however, these have not been obtained. The reason may be that Kotovsky and Gentner (1996) provided feedback during the training trials. Thus, children might show progressive alignment effects in a number experiment if they received feedback on their literal similarity matches.

In summary, there are several conceptual links between number and categorization. Number applies to that which has been categorized, and numbers themselves can be construed as categories. Therefore, it would not be surprising to find developmental links between these areas of competence. For example, the ability to evaluate quantity may depend on an ability to form other kinds of categories. Further, the development of numerical equivalence judgments may be affected by the same kinds of input as other kinds of comparisons.

Language

Although children exhibit many quantitative skills before they know the words for numbers or mathematical concepts, acquiring mathematical language opens the door to new ways of thinking and complex skills, as we have pointed out. An understanding of complex concepts, such as those involved in calculus, almost certainly depends on mastery of mathematical symbols. Indeed, the impact of new symbol systems on quantitative thought has been documented throughout the history of mathematics.

Of course, language effects are not unique to mathematics. Research on the development of other concepts documents similar findings. For example, infants and children who know the names for categories are more likely to group objects taxonomically (Baldwin & Markman, 1989; Markman & Hutchinson, 1984; Waxman & Hall, 1993; Waxman & Markow, 1995). That is, children who learn the word "bowl" are more likely to pair two bowls than to match a bowl with a spoon. Likewise, children who know a word for an attribute, such as a color or pattern, are more likely to group disparate items accordingly (Smith, 1993). In fact, recent longitudinal research suggests that learning adjectives precedes dimensional matching for some properties (Sandhofer & Smith, 1999). Specifically, children know the words for colors before they can match items of the same color. Furthermore, children recognize relational similarity and infer common characteristics for items that have the same name (Gelman & Markman, 1987; Gentner, Rattermann, Markman, & Kotovsky, 1995). It is thought that these language effects arise because words alert children to possible commonalities between items and help to focus their attention (Sandhofer & Smith, 1999; Waxman & Markow, 1995). For example, hearing an apple and a truck called "red" tells children that these two items have something in common. Given some experience with color words, this labeling might also focus children's attention on the dimension of color.

Count words could play a similar role. We know that children spontaneously label numerical sets in the normal course of number development. Wagner and Walters (1982) found that children's first uses of the count words "two" and "three" were unaccompanied by counting. Wynn (1990, 1992) also reported that children first learn the names for sets of 1, 2, and 3 items before understanding that the last word in a count stands for the cardinal value of the set. In our research, we have observed that children often call out number words during numerical equivalence tasks. Frequently these words are nowhere near the actual size of the sets being presented (e.g., saying "17" in the presence of two dots), but it is interesting that children attempt to use a label in this context, especially a label from the correct domain. Others have reported similar observations. Baroody (1998) relates the story of his daughter, Arianne, who initially answered, "two," whenever she was asked how many things were in a set, no matter what number of items the sets actually contained. It is as if children treat numbers like any other category that can take a name. Moreover, these errors are reminiscent of children's overgeneralizations of other classes of words. Just as children must learn that the word "dog" does not apply to all four-legged animals, they must learn that the number "two" does not apply to all numerosities.

If the count words function like other category names, then the naming of sets should affect quantitative development just as it does for other concepts. Knowing the first few count words might organize attention toward number and help children see sets as numerically equivalent. It also might promote abstraction by hinting at a basis for grouping sets that are otherwise different. Indeed, simply knowing that words signal commonalities in other situations may give children the expectation that number words work the same way. This powerful insight would help children transcend their preverbal representations of quantity. Similar effects might hold for other kinds of mathematical language, such as words for arithmetical operations, fractions, and measurement. For example, once children can recognize the term "one-half," it might lead them to analyze more closely how different quantities called one-half are alike.

Language could also affect quantitative development as a memory aid. Although children can represent quantity before they learn to count, these nonverbal representations have significant limitations. They work only for sets up to 4 or 5 items; they do not extend easily to sequential sets, and so forth. Of course, verbal counting does not have these drawbacks in principle. Although children learn the meanings of small numbers first, learning to count eventually gives children a way to remember the exact number in an infinite range of set sizes.

This memory advantage undoubtedly improves calculation as well. When children use a mental model to perform simple calculation, there is much information to keep in memory. They must first construct a mental version of each item. They must remember the direction of the transformation and the number of items involved. Finally, they have to keep the resulting number of items in mind while they construct a solution. There are no opportunities for reminders because the problems are sequential events. That is, once the number of items has been transformed, no information about the starting point is perceptually available.

With verbal problems, (e.g., "What is five plus three?") the number words serve as reminders of the stages of the transformation, so there is no need to reconstruct the entire event in memory. For example, if children were unsure about the starting amount, they need only recall the word "five" rather than remember each individual item in the initial set. Although they might still need to reconstruct this set mentally or using fingers until they have mastered the number facts, the count word would nonetheless serve as a intermediate marker that probably requires less memory than recalling each item. This memory advantage could be even greater when written symbols, such as $5 + 3 = ?$, are used because this changes the problems from sequential events to static representations. Thus, for written problems, the whole sequence is summarized and the various parts can be reviewed as needed.

So far we have focused on the possible effects of language acquisition on quantitative development. However, learning mathematical words might also influence children's ideas about language. One potential influence is the idea that words can refer to sets and properties of sets. For English speakers, most early words are object names (Nelson, 1973). In fact, children are strongly biased to interpret new words in terms of whole objects rather than parts, and in terms of overall shape rather than other features (Baldwin, 1989; Jones, Smith, & Landau, 1991; Markman & Wachtel, 1988; Soja, Carey, & Spelke, 1991; Waxman & Senghas, 1992). When children learn the number words, they are exposed to the idea that words can name groups as well as individual objects.

Given children's bias to learn words that refer to objects, learning number words should not be an easy task—not only because the number words refer to groups but also because they refer to *properties* of groups. Previous research has shown that children acquire property terms, such as color, texture, and pattern words, with more difficulty than they acquire object names (Carey, 1982; Nelson, 1973; Smith & Sera, 1992). Even among property terms, the words for number may be especially difficult because they refer to a property that emerges from a grouping rather than pertaining inherently to an individual. For example, a red apple is red whether or not it is grouped together with other apples. However, three apples are only three apples when they are grouped somehow (i.e., spatially, temporally, or both).

Indeed, there is evidence that number words are more difficult to learn than words for object properties, such as color. In a novel word-learning task given to 4-year-olds, Mix and Waxman (1999) found that, across training conditions, children performed less well learning novel number words than learning novel color words. This pattern also was reflected in children's mastery of the familiar English words. When asked to either select a block of a particular color (e.g., "Give me the brown block") or produce a particular set size (e.g., "Give me three blocks"), 4-year-olds' receptive color vocabulary was significantly better than their number vocabulary. Thus, in their everyday environments, children appear to find learning color words easier than number words, perhaps because color words refer to a property of objects, whereas number words refer to a property of sets.

Although acquiring number vocabulary may be especially difficult, once learned it could provide the foundation for understanding other classes of words that name sets, such as collective nouns (e.g., family, forest, flock) and collective adjectives (e.g., bustling city, crowded mall, mountainous terrain). Although this hypothesis has not been tested directly, it is at least consistent with the age trends observed in collective noun acquisition. Bloom and Kelemen (1995) taught adults, 4-, and 5-year-olds novel names for groups of animals and machines. The critical manipulation was that some children learned a plural noun for the group (e.g., "These are fendles") and others learned a collective noun (e.g., "This is a fendle"). At test, children were asked which of two pictures—one with another group of objects from the training set and one with a single object from the training set—showed the novel noun (e.g., "Can you show me the fendle?"). If subjects interpreted the singular noun as referring to a collection, then they should pick the group at test. Bloom and Kelemen observed a gradual increase in this construal over the three age groups. Although 4-year-olds performed at chance, an inspection of the means revealed that those who learned the collective noun tended to pick the group of items more often than the individual item at test. By age 5, children reliably chose the syntactic match, an effect even stronger at adulthood. Thus, attention to the syntax of collective nouns seems to emerge between 4 and 5 years of age. We know that children learn the meanings of small numbers around 3 years of age and have discovered the cardinal word principle (i.e., the last word in a count stands for the numerosity of the set) by 4 years of age (Wynn, 1990, 1992). This may be no coincidence. Indeed, Bloom and Kelemen speculated that "the gradual increase in collective responses with age might be due to an increasing ability to construe the groups as collections" (p. 25). We propose here that the ability to see groups as collections may be promoted by learning to name groups with count words.

Of course, this is not the only possible relation between counting, number concepts, and collection terms. Indeed, Markman (1979) showed that 4½-year-olds were more likely to conserve number when sets were labeled with collective nouns (e.g., "What's more, your army, my army, or are they both the same?"). Thus, using collection nouns focused children's attention on the set-level property of number, thereby facilitating numerical reasoning in an otherwise difficult task.

Learning mathematical language might also help children understand the relation between spoken language and written symbols. Both written numerals and words are arbitrary patterns that stand for a spoken word. However, one could argue that the relation between numerals and number words is more transparent because, at least up to 9, each spoken word is represented by one unique symbol (e.g., the numeral 3 represents the spoken word three). This one-to-one mapping would allow children to connect these symbol systems by simple association—one distinct symbol paired with another. Number words are unusual because they have this intervening symbol between the spoken word and written word. For other words the connection between speech and print is more complex. Written words result from combining discrete symbols that stand for individual sounds. Thus, even though each word is a unique symbol, its constituents appear across many other words. If children cannot easily tell one word from another because the words share common parts, they would find forming associations with a spoken equivalent difficult.

Of course, learning to read involves much more than simply associating whole written words with whole spoken words. It requires children to learn the sound-symbol relations at the letter level—in effect decomposing the spoken words into parts and associating these parts with symbolic equivalents. This process ultimately imparts great flexibility by providing a way to decode even unfamiliar words. However, these individual sounds are rarely uttered in isolation. Furthermore, the relation between sounds and letters is often many-to-one (e.g., hard "c" and soft "c"). Because the mappings between spoken count words and single-digit numerals are so straightforward, learning them may set the stage for reading in a way that letter-sound pairings cannot, by introducing the idea that a written symbol can stand for a spoken word.

Space

The ties between spatial and quantitative development may not be obvious at first. After all, reading a road map does not seem to have much in common with solving algebraic equations. However, research with young children suggests that prior to acquisition of these formal skills, the domains of space and number are closely related. In fact, the quantification of infants and young children could be accurately termed "spatial quantification."

This view is supported by mounting evidence that infants see quantities in terms of overall amount rather than discrete number. We have argued that infants use relative amount in particular (i.e., the amount of stuff relative to its container) because absolute amount cannot be represented accurately without conventional measurement. If so, these early estimates of amount might well be based on the same metrics used in spatial reasoning, such as length relative to a landmark, proportion of area, and so forth. In other words, the same information that tells you how far across a room you will find your favorite toy can also tell you how much juice is in a glass or how much of a plate is covered with cookies.

If space and number share common perceptual and representational origins, then developmental parallels between the two domains should be evident. Earlier, we pointed out one commonality. Gao et al. (2000) found that infants dishabituate to changes in the amount of liquid in a clear cylinder. A parallel finding from spatial development is that infants recognized when hidden objects emerged from incorrect locations in a sandbox by estimating the distance from the edge (Newcombe et al., 1999). These tasks seem to require the same competence: representation of relative amount.

Additional evidence of a link between space and quantity comes from research showing developmental deficits in the two domains. Several researchers (Semrud-Clikeman & Hynd, 1990; Spiers, 1987) have suggested that visuo-spatial deficits in childhood may be especially detrimental to the development of basic numerical skills. In fact, studies of learning-disabled populations support the existence of a spatially mediated type of arithmetic deficit. For example, children with selective arithmetic deficits performed significantly worse on the WISC Performance Scale than patients with both arithmetic and language deficits (Rourke & Finlayson, 1978; Share, Moffitt, & Silva, 1988). Consistent with these findings, other studies report an association between arithmetic deficits in children and right hemisphere dysfunction (Gross-Tsur, Shalev, Manor, & Amir, 1995; Tranel, Hall, Olson, & Tranel, 1987).

McClean and Hitch (1999) found that children with poor arithmetic skills also show deficits in spatio-temporal memory. In their study, 9-year-olds with specific arithmetic disabilities (i.e., normal verbal and reading skills) were given a battery of memory tests. The goal was to determine what particular aspects of working memory were related to children's difficulty learning arithmetic. Compared to age-matched controls, children with arithmetic disabilities performed significantly worse on several visuo-spatial tasks, suggesting that one underlying problem in this population is poor spatio-temporal working memory.

This pattern is also evident in children with Williams Syndrome, a genetic disorder. These children have a characteristic cognitive profile;

their language skills and auditory memory are relatively strong, but they exhibit severe impairment on visuo-spatial construction tasks (Morris & Mervis, 1999). Academically, they manage to acquire basic reading and spelling skills but have great difficulty learning mathematics (Howlin, Davies, & Udwin, 1998). Thus, children with Williams Syndrome exhibit specific impairments in both spatial and mathematical skills.

These studies hint at a close developmental link between mathematics and spatial ability—children who lack adequate spatial skills have trouble learning mathematics. This connection may arise when conventional skills are acquired. For example, children who lack spatial skills may start to have trouble when they must represent the number line or multiplication tables. However, if we are correct in concluding that early quantification is essentially a spatial process, then the origins of these arithmetic deficits may be much earlier. Children who lack the common starting point for spatial reasoning and quantification would also lack the preverbal foundation onto which mathematical conventions are normally mapped.

Although spatial and quantitative skills may have common developmental origins, there is likely to be divergence once children learn conventional skills (Newcombe & Huttenlocher, in press). Conventional skills may have a greater impact on the development of number concepts. Conventions allow children to perform operations over much larger quantities than the preverbal system allows. Conventions may also serve as catalysts of conceptual change, as when children learn about the importance of equal units by learning to measure. In contrast, the ability to navigate reliably emerges early and without conventional skills. Thus, whereas spatial conventions may formalize children's existing representations, they probably do not alter spatial behavior significantly (Newcombe & Huttenlocher, in press).

Still, connections between space and number endure even in adulthood. Many of the conventions used in spatial tasks have a mathematical component. For example, reading or producing a map requires an understanding of scale (i.e., the mathematical ratio between actual space and represented space). Furthermore, there is evidence of a spatial component in adults' representations of number. Dehaene (1997) found that when adults were asked to judge whether a number was larger or smaller than 65, they responded faster and more accurately for small sets with their left hands and large sets with their right hands. This effect, dubbed the Spatial-Numerical Association of Response Codes, or SNARC effect, suggested that adults represent quantities according to positions on a number line. Of course, the SNARC effect reflects a very different sort of spatial representation than that used by infants. Indeed, it seems to develop through exposure to culture-specific counting and reading conventions (i.e., the effect reverses in adults who read from right to left). Nonetheless, it is interesting to note the pervasive intermingling of these two domains.

Conclusions

The connections across areas we have examined in this chapter highlight how intricately quantitative development is linked to other aspects of cognitive growth. These relations are not unidirectional—just as quantitative development is promoted by growth in many areas of cognition, it also has a significant affect on development in these other areas. This is a fitting way to end our examination of early quantitative development because it reminds us that the issues raised here are important not only to researchers interested in quantitative concepts. Instead, the way quantitative development is conceptualized can have far-reaching theoretical implications. We hope that this book has inspired new ways of thinking about early quantification that will initiate a rich scientific dialogue both within the field of quantitative development and beyond.

References

Antell, S., & Keating, D. P. (1983). Perception of numerical invariance in neonates. *Child Development, 54*, 695–701.

Ashcraft, M. H. (1982). The development of mental arithmetic: A chronometric approach. *Developmental Review, 2*, 213–236.

Baldwin, D. (1989). Priorities in children's expectations about object label reference: Form over color. *Child Development, 60*, 1291–1306.

Baldwin, D., & Markman, E. M. (1989). Establishing word-object relations: A first step. *Child Development, 60*, 381–398.

Baroody, A. J. (1987). *Children's mathematical thinking: A developmental framework for preschool, primary, and special education teachers*. New York: Teachers College Press.

Baroody, A. J. (1992). The development of preschoolers' counting skills and principles. In J. Bideaud, C. Meljac, & J. Fischer (Eds.), *Pathways to number: Children's developing numerical abilities* (pp. 99–126). Hillsdale, NJ: Erlbaum.

Baroody, A. J. (1998). *Fostering children's mathematical power: An investigative approach to K–8 mathematics instruction*. Mahwah, NJ: Erlbaum.

Baroody, A. J., & Ginsburg, H. (1986). The relationship between initial meaningful and mechanical knowledge of arithmetic. In J. Hiebert (Ed.), *Conceptual and procedural knowledge: The case of mathematics* (pp. 75–112). Hillsdale, NJ: Erlbaum.

Baroody, A. J., & Price, J. (1983). The development of the number-word sequence in the counting of three-year-olds. *Journal for Research in Mathematics Education, 14*, 361–368.

Baroody, A. J., Tiilikainen, S. H., & Liao, H. (in press). The development of adaptive expertise and flexibility: The integration of conceptual and procedural knowledge. In A. J. Baroody & A. Dowker (Eds.), *The develop-ment of arithmetic concepts and skills: Constructing adaptive expertise*. Mah-wah, NJ: Erlbaum.

Behr, M. J., Lesh, R., Post, T. R., & Silver, E. A. (1983). Rational number con-cepts. In R. Lesh & M. Landau (Eds.) *Acquisition of mathematics concepts and processes* (pp. 91–126). New York: Academic

Behr, M. J., Wachsmuth, I., Post, T. R., & Lesh, R. (1984). Order and equiva-lence: A clinical teaching experiment. *Journal for Research in Mathematics Education, 15*(5), 323–341.

Bloom, P., & Kelemen, D. (1995). Syntactic cues in the acquisition of collective nouns. *Cognition, 56*, 1–30.

Braine, M. D. S. (1959). The ontogeny of certain logical operations: Piaget's formulation examined by nonverbal methods. *Psychological Monographs, 73*(5, whole no. 475).

Brainerd, C. J. (1973a). Mathematical and behavioral foundations of number. *Journal of General Psychology, 88*, 221–281.

Brainerd, C. J. (1973b). The origins of number concepts. *Scientific American, 228*(3), 101–109.

Brainerd, C. J., & Fraser, M. (1975). A further test of the ordinal theory of number development. *Journal of Genetic Psychology, 127*, 21–33.

Brannon, E., & Van de Walle, G. (1999, April). *Knowledge of numerical ordinal relations in 2- to 3-year-olds*. Poster presented at the biennial meeting of the Society for Research in Child Development, Albuquerque, New Mexico.

Briars, D. J., & Siegler, R. S. (1984). A featural analysis of preschoolers' count-ing knowledge. *Developmental Psychology, 20*, 607–618.

Bruner, J. S., Olver, R. R., Greenfield, P. M., et al. (1966). *Studies in cognitive growth*. New York: Wiley.

Bryant, P. (1974). *Perception and understanding in young children*. London: Methuen.

Bullock, M., & Gelman, R. (1977). Numerical reasoning in young children: The ordering principle. *Child Development, 48*, 427–434.

Canfield, R. L., & Smith, E. G. (1996). Number-based expectations and se-quential enumeration by 5-month-old infants. *Developmental Psychology, 32*(2) , 269–279.

Carey, S. (1982). Semantic development: The state of the art. In L. R. Gleit-man and E. Wanner (Eds.), *Language acquisition: The state of the art*. Cam-bridge: Cambridge University Press.

Carpenter, T. P., & Moser, J. M. (1982). The development of addition and sub-traction problem solving. In T. P. Carpenter, J. M. Moser, and T. A. Romberg (Eds.), (pp. 9–24). *Rational numbers: An integration of research*. Hillsdale, NJ: Erlbaum.

Case, R. (1985). *Intellectual development: Birth to adulthood*. New York: Academic.

Chi, M. T. H., & Klahr, D. (1975). Span and rate of apprehension in children and adults. *Journal of Experimental Child Psychology, 19*, 157–192.

Choi, S., & Bowerman, M. (1991). Learning to express motion events in En-glish and Korean: The influence of language-specific lexicalization pat-terns. *Cognition, 41*, 83–121.

Clearfield, M. W., & Mix, K. S. (1999). Number versus contour length in infants' discrimination of small visual sets. *Psychological Science, 10,* 408–411.

Clearfield, M. W., & Mix, K. S. (2000). *Amount versus number: Infants' use of area and contour length to discriminate small sets.* Unpublished manuscript.

Cohen, L. B., & Younger, B. A. (1983). Perceptual categorization in the infant. In E. K. Scholnick (Ed.) *New trends in conceptual representation: Challenges to Piaget's Theory?* (pp. 197–220). Hillsdale, NJ: Erlbaum.

Cooper, R. G. Jr. (1984). Early number development: Discovering number space with addition and subtraction. In C. Sophian (Ed.), *Origins of cognitive skills.* (pp. 157–192). Hillsdale, NJ: Erlbaum.

Correa, J. (1995). *Young children's understanding of the division concept.* Unpublished dissertation, University of Oxford.

Curtis, L. E., & Strauss, M. S. (1982). *Development of numerosity discrimination abilities.* Paper presented at the meetings of the International Conference of Infant Studies, Austin, Texas.

Curtis, L. E., & Strauss, M. S. (1983). *Infant numerosity abilities: Discrimination and relative numerosity.* Paper presented at the meetings of the Society for Research in Child Development, Detroit, Michigan.

Danzig, T. (1967). *Number: The language of science.* New York: Free Press.

Davis, H. (1984). Discrimination of the number three by a raccoon (Pryocyon lotor). *Animal Learning and Behavior, 12,* 409–413.

Davis, H., & Perusse, R. (1988). Numerical competence in animals: Definitional issues, current evidence, and a new research agenda. *Behavioral and Brain Sciences, 11,* 561–615.

Dehaene, S. (1997). *The number sense: How the mind creates mathematics.* New York: Oxford University Press.

DeLoache, J. S. (1987). Rapid change in the symbolic functioning of very young children. *Science, 238,* 1556–1557.

DeLoache, J. S. (1989). The development of representation in young children. In H. W. Reese (Ed.), *Advances in child development and behavior* (vol. 22, pp. 1–39). New York: Academic Press.

DeLoache, J. S. (1991). Symbolic functioning in very young children: Understanding of picture models. *Child Development, 62,* 736–752.

Demany, L., McKenzie, B., & Vurpillot, E. (1977, April). Rhythm perception in early infancy. *Nature, 266,* 718–719.

Dixon, R. M. W. (1980). *The languages of Australia.* Cambridge: Cambridge University Press.

Donaldson, M., & Wales, R. J. (1970). On the acquisition of some relational terms. In J. R. Hayes (Ed.), *Cognition and the development of language* (pp. 235–268). New York: Wiley.

Douglass, H. R. (1925). The development of the number concept in children of preschool and kindergarten ages. *Journal of Experimental Psychology, 8,* 443–470.

Fantz, R. L., & Fagan, J. F. (1975). Visual attention to size and number of pattern details by term and preterm infants during the first six months. *Child Development, 46,* 3–18.

Feigenson, L., & Spelke, E. (1998). *Numerical knowledge in infancy: The num-*

ber/mass distinction. Poster presented at the meetings of the International Conference on Infant Studies, Atlanta, Georgia.

Fischer, F. E., & Beckey, R. D. (1990). Beginning kindergarteners' perception of number. *Perceptual and Motor Skills, 70*, 419–425.

Freeman, K., & Goswami, U. (1997, April). *Does half a pizza equal half a dozen? Good analogies for introducing fractions to preschoolers*. Poster presented at the biennial meeting of the Society for Research in Child Development, Washington, DC.

Frydman, O., & Bryant, P. (1988). Sharing and the understanding of number equivalence by young children. *Cognitive Development, 3*, 323–339.

Frye, D., Braisby, N., Lowe, J., Maroudas, C., & Nichols, J. (1989). Young children's understanding of counting and cardinality. *Child Development, 60*, 1158–1171.

Fuson, K. C. (1988). *Children's counting and conceptions of number*. New York: Springer-Verlag.

Gallistel, C. R., & Gelman, R. (1992). Preverbal and verbal counting and computation. *Cognition, 44*, 43–74.

Gao, F., Huttenlocher, J., & Levine, S.C. (in preparation). *Addition of discrete and continuous quantities in preschool children*.

Gao, F., Levine, S. C., & Huttenlocher, J. (2000). What do infants know about continuous quantity? *Journal of Experimental Child Psychology, 77*, 20–29

Gelman, R. (1969). Conservation acquisition: A problem of learning to attend to relevant attributes. *Journal of Experimental Child Psychology, 7*, 67–87.

Gelman R. (1972). Logical capacity in very young children. *Child Development, 43*, 75–90.

Gelman, R. (1991). Epigenetic foundations of knowledge structures: Initial and transcendent constructions. In S. Carey & R. Gelman. (Eds.), *Epigenesis of mind: Essays on biology and cognition* (pp. 293–322). Hillsdale, NJ: Erlbaum.

Gelman, R., & Brenneman, K. (1994). First principles can support both universal and culture-specific learning about number and music. In L. A. Hirschfeld & S. A. Gelman (Eds.), *Mapping the mind: Domain specificity in cognition and culture*. New York: Cambridge University Press.

Gelman, R., & Gallistel, C. R. (1978). *The child's understanding of number*. Cambridge, MA: Harvard University Press.

Gelman, S. A., & Markman, E. M. (1987). Young children's induction from natural kinds: The role of categories and appearances. *Child Development, 58*, 1532–1541.

Gelman, R., & Meck, E. (1983). Preschoolers' counting: Principles before skill. *Cognition, 13*, 343–359.

Gentner, D., & Rattermann, M. J. (1991). Language and the career of similarity. In S. A. Gelman & J. P. Byrnes (Eds.), *Perspectives on language and thought: Interrelations in development* (pp. 225–277). London: Cambridge University Press.

Gentner, D., Rattermann, M. J., Markman, A., & Kotovsky, L. (1995). Two forces in the development of relational similarity. In T. J. Simon, G. S. Halford, et al. (Eds.) *Developing cognitive competence: New Approaches to process modeling* (pp. 263–313). Hillsdale, NJ: Erlbaum.

Gentner, D., & Toupin, C. (1986). Systematicity and surface similarity in the development of analogy. *Cognitive Science, 10*, 277–300.

Gibson, E. J. (1969). *Principles of perceptual learning and development.* New York: Appleton-Century-Crofts.

Glasersfeld, E. von (1982). Subitizing: The role of figural patterns in the development of numerical concepts. *Archives de Psychologie, 50*, 191–218.

Goldstein, D., Hasher, L., & Stein, D. K. (1983). The processing of occurrence rate and item information by children of different ages and abilities. *American Journal of Psychology, 96*, 229–241.

Goswami, U. (1989). Relational complexity and the development of analogical reasoning. *Cognitive Development, 4*, 251–268.

Groen, G. J., & Parkman, J. M. (1972). A chronometric analysis of simple addition. *Psychological Review, 79*, 329–343.

Gross-Tsur, V., Shalev, R. S., Manor, O., & Amir, N. (1995). Developmental right-hemisphere syndrome: Clinical spectrum of the nonverbal learning disability. *Journal of Learning Disabilities, 28*, 80–86.

Hasher, L., & Chromiak, W. (1977). The processing of frequency information: An automatic mechanism? *Journal of Verbal Learning and Verbal Behavior, 16*, 173–184.

Hasher, L., & Zacks, R. T. (1979). Automatic and effortful processes in memory. *Journal of Experimental Psychology: General, 108*, 356–388.

Hasher, L., & Zacks, R. T. (1984). Automatic processing of fundamental information: The case for frequency of occurrence. *American Psychologist, 39*, 1372–1388.

Holyoak, K. J., Junn, E. N., & Billman, D. O. (1984). Development of analogical problem-solving skill. *Child Development, 55*, 2042–2055.

Howlin, P., Davies, M., & Udwin, U. (1998). Syndrome specific characteristics in Williams syndrome: To what extent do early behavioural patterns persist into adult life? *Journal of Applied Research in Intellectual Disabilities, 11*, 207–226.

Hughes, M. (1981). Can preschool children add and subtract? *Educational Psychology, 1*, 207–219.

Hughes, M. (1986). *Children and number.* Oxford: Blackwell.

Hunting, R. P. (1986). Rachel's schemes for constructing fraction knowledge. *Educational Studies in Mathematics, 17*, 49–66.

Hunting, R. P., & Davis, G. E. (1991) *Dimensions of young children's conceptions of the fraction one half: Early fraction learning.* New York: Springer-Verlag.

Hunting, R. P., & Sharpley, C. F. (1988). Preschoolers' cognitions of fractional units. *British Journal of Educational Psychology, 58*, 172–183.

Huntley-Fenner, G. N. (1999, April). *The effect of material kind on preschoolers' judgments of quantity.* Poster presented at the biennial meeting of the Society for Research in Child Development, Albuquerque, New Mexico.

Huntley-Fenner, G. N., & Carey, S. E. (1995). *Individuation of objects and portions of nonsolid substances: A pattern of success (objects) and failure (nonsolid substances).* Paper presented at the biennial meeting of the Society for Research in Child Development, Indianapolis, Indiana.

Huttenlocher, J. (1994, November). *The emergence of number.* Paper presented at the annual meeting of the Psychonomic Society, St. Louis, Missouri.

Huttenlocher, J., Jordan, N., & Levine, S. C. (1994). A mental model for early arithmetic. *Journal of Experimental Psychology: General, 123*, 284–296.

Huttenlocher, J., Newcombe, N., & Vasilyeva, M. (1999). Spatial scaling in young children. *Psychological Science, 10* (5), 393–398.

Jensen, E. M., Reese, E. P., & Reese, T. W. (1950). The subitizing and counting of visually presented fields of dots. *Journal of Psychology, 30*, 363–392.

Jevons, W. (1871). The power of numerical discrimination. *Nature, 3*, 281–282.

Jones, S., Smith, L., & Landau, B. (1991). Object properties and knowledge in early lexical learning. *Child Development, 62*, 499–516.

Jeong, Y. K., Levine, S. C., & Huttenlocher, J. (In preparation) *Children's development of probability reasoning*.

Jordan, N. C., Huttenlocher, J., & Levine, S. C. (1994). Assessing early arithmetic abilities: Effects of verbal and nonverbal response types on the calculation performance of middle- and low-income children. *Learning and Individual Differences, 6*, 413–432.

Kahneman, D., Triesman, A., & Gibbs, B. J. (1992). The reviewing of object files: Object specific integration of information. *Cognitive Psychology, 24*, 175–219.

Karmiloff-Smith, A. (1992). *Beyond modularity: A developmental perspective on cognitive science*. Cambridge, MA: MIT Press/Bradford Books.

Kaufman, E. L., Lord, M. W., Reese, T. W., & Volkmann, J. (1949). The discrimination of visual number. *American Journal of Psychology, 62*, 498–525.

Kellman, P. J., & Banks, M. S. (1998). Infant visual perception. In W. Damon (Ed.) & D. Kuhn and R. S. Siegler (Vol. Eds.), *Handbook of child psychology: Vol. 2. Cognition, perception, and language* (5th ed., pp. 103–146). New York: Wiley.

Kellman, P. J., & Spelke, E. S. (1983). Perception of partly occluded objects in infancy. *Cognitive Psychology, 15*, 483–524.

Kerslake, D. (1986). Fractions: Children's strategies and errors. *A Report of the Strategies and Errors in Secondary Mathematics Project*. Windsor, England: NFER-NELSON.

Klahr, D. (1973). Quantification processes. In W. G. Chase (Ed.), *Visual information processing* (pp. 3–34). New York: Academic Press.

Klahr, D., & Wallace, J. G. (1976). *Cognitive development: An information-processing approach*. Hillsdale, NJ: Erlbaum.

Klibanoff, R. S., & Waxman, S. R. (2000). Basic level object categories support the acquisition of novel adjectives: Evidence from preschool children. *Child Development, 71*, 649–659.

Kotovsky, L., & Gentner, D. (1996). Comparison and categorization in the development of relational similarity. *Child Development, 67*, 2797–2822.

Levine, S. C., Jeong, Y. K., & Gao, F. (1999, April). Is it harder to quantify discrete entities or continuous amounts? In J. Huttenlocher (Chair), *Concepts of continuous amount*. Symposium conducted at the biennial meeting of the Society for Research in Child Development, Albuquerque, New Mexico.

Levine, S. C., Jordan, N. C., & Huttenlocher, J. (1992). Development of calculation abilities in young children. *Journal of Experimental Child Psychology, 53*, 72–103.

Lovett, S. B., & Singer, J. (1991, April). *The development of children's understanding of probability: Perceptual and quantitative conceptions.* Poster presented at the biennial meeting of the Society for Research in Child Development, Seattle, Washington.

Mack, N. (1990). Learning fractions with understanding: Building on informal knowledge. *Journal for Research in Mathematics Education, 21*(1), 16–32.

Mack, N. (1993). Learning rational numbers with understanding: The case of informal knowledge. In T. P. Carpenter, J. M. Moser, & T. A. Romberg (Eds.), *Rational numbers: An integration of research* (pp. 85–106). Hillsdale, NJ: Erlbaum.

Mandler, G., & Shebo, B. J. (1982). Subitizing: An analysis of its component processes. *Journal of Experimental Psychology: General, 11,* 1–22.

Mandler, J., & Bauer, P. J. (1988). The cradle of categorization: Is the basic level basic? *Cognitive Development, 3*(3), 247–264.

Markman, E. M. (1979). Classes and collections: Conceptual organization and numerical abilities. *Cognitive Psychology, 11,* 395–411.

Markman, E. M., & Hutchinson, J. E., (1984). Children's sensitivity to constraints in word meaning: Taxonomic versus thematic relations. *Cognitive Psychology, 16,* 1–27.

Markman, E. M., & Wachtel, G. F. (1988). Children's use of mutual exclusivity to constrain the meaning of words. *Cognitive Psychology, 20,* 121–157.

McCall, R. B., & Kagan, J. (1967). Attention in the infant: Effects of complexity, contour, perimeter, and familiarity. *Child Development, 38,* 939–952.

McCune-Nicolich, L. (1981). Toward symbolic functioning: Structure of early pretend games and potential parallels with language. *Child Development, 52,* 785–797.

McLean, J. F., & Hitch, G. J. (1999). Working memory impairments in children with specific arithmetic learning difficulties. *Journal of Experimental Child Psychology, 74,* 240–260.

Mechner, F. (1958). Probability relations within response sequences under ration reinforcement. *Journal of Experimental Analysis of Behavior, 1,* 109–122.

Meck, W. H., & Church, R. M. (1983). A mode control model of counting and timing processes. *Journal of Experimental Psychology: Animal Behavior Processes, 9,* 320–334.

Mehler, J., & Bever, T. G. (1967). Cognitive capacity of very young children. *Science, 158,* 141–142.

Miller, K. F. (1984). Child as measurer of all things: Measurement procedures and the development of quantitative concepts. In C. Sophian (Ed.), *Origins of cognitive skills* (pp. 193–228). Hillsdale, NJ: Erlbaum.

Miller, K. F. (1992). What a number is: Mathematical foundations and developing number concepts. In J. I. D. Campbell (Ed.), *The nature and origins of mathematical skills* (pp. 3–38). New York: Elsevier.

Miller, K. F., & Stigler, J. W. (1987). Counting in Chinese: Variation in a basic cognitive skill. *Cognitive Development, 2,* 279–305.

Mix, K. S. (1999a). Preschoolers' recognition of numerical equivalence: Sequential sets. *Journal of Experimental Child Psychology, 74,* 309–332.

Mix, K. S. (1999b). Similarity and numerical equivalence: Appearances count. *Cognitive Development, 14*, 269–297.

Mix, K. S. (in preparation). *The emergence of number-based responses in quantitative equivalence tasks.*

Mix, K. S., Huttenlocher, J., & Levine, S. C. (1996). Do preschool children recognize auditory-visual numerical correspondences? *Child Development, 67*, 1592–1608.

Mix, K. S., Huttenlocher, J., & Levine, S. C. (in preparation). *Preschoolers' comparisons of fractions.*

Mix, K. S., Levine, S. C., & Huttenlocher, J. (1997). Numerical abstraction in infants: Another look. *Developmental Psychology, 33 (3)*, 423–428.

Mix, K. S., Levine, S. C., & Huttenlocher, J. (1999). Early fraction calculation ability. *Developmental Psychology, 35*(1), 164–174.

Mix, K. S., & Waxman, S. (1999, October). *Are color concepts easier to learn than number concepts?* Poster presented at the first annual meeting of the Cognitive Development Society, Chapel Hill, North Carolina.

Moore, D., Benenson, J., Reznick, J. S., Peterson, M., & Kagan, J. (1987). Effect of auditory numerical information on infants' looking behavior: Contradictory evidence. *Developmental Psychology, 23*, 665–670.

Morris, C. A., & Mervis, C. B. (1999). Williams syndrome. In S. Goldstein, C. R. Reynolds, et al. (Eds.). *Handbook of neurodevelopmental and genetic disorders in children* (pp. 555–590). New York: Guilford Press.

Nelson, K. (1973). Structure and strategy in learning to talk. *Monographs for the Society of Research in Child Development, 38*(1–2, Serial No. 149).

Newcombe, N., & Huttenlocher, J. (in press). *Making space: The development of spatial representation and reasoning.*

Newcombe, N., Huttenlocher, J., & Learmonth, A. (1999). Infants' coding of location in continuous space. *Infant Behavior and Development, 22*(4), 483–510.

Nunes, T., & Bryant, P. (1996). *Children doing mathematics.* Cambridge, MA: Blackwell.

Nunes, T., Light, P., & Mason, J. (1993). Tools for thought: The measurement of length and area. *Learning and Instruction, 3*, 39–54.

Oakes, L. M., Madole, K. L., & Cohen, L. B. (1991). Infants' object examining: Habituation and categorization. *Cognitive Development, 6*, 377–392.

Petitto, A. L. (1990) Development of numberline and measurement concepts. *Cognition and Instruction, 7*(1), 55–78.

Piaget, J. (1941/1965). *The child's conception of number.* New York: Norton.

Piaget, J., & Inhelder, B. (1975). *The origin of the idea of chance in children.* New York: Norton.

Platt, J. R., & Johnson, D. M. (1971). Localization of position within a homogeneous behavior chain: Effects of error contigencies. *Learning and Motivation, 2*, 386–414.

Resnick, L. B., & Ford, W. W. (1981). *The psychology of mathematics for instruction.* Hillsdale, NJ: Erlbaum.

Rittle-Johnson, B., & Siegler, R. S. (1998). The relation between conceptual and procedural knowledge in learning mathematics: A review of the literature. In C. Donlan (Ed.), *The development of mathematical skills* (pp. 75–110). Hove, England: Psychology Press.

Ross, G. S. (1980). Categorization in 1- to 2-year-olds. *Developmental Psychology, 16*, 391–396.

Rothenberg, B. B. (1969). Conservation of number among 4- and 5-year-old children: Some methodological considerations. *Child Development, 40,* 383–406.

Rourke, B. P., & Finlayson, M. A. (1978). Neuropsychological significance of variations in patterns of academic performance: Verbal and visual-spatial abilities. *Journal of Abnormal Child Psychology, 6*, 121–133.

Russell, B. (1919/1993). *Introduction to mathematical philosophy.* New York: Dover.

Sandhofer, C. M., & Smith, L. B. (1999). Learning color words involves learning a system of mappings. *Developmental Psychology, 35*, 668–679.

Schaeffer, B., Eggleston, V. H., & Scott, J. L. (1974). Number development in young children. *Cognitive Psychology, 6*, 357–379.

Semrud-Clikeman, M., & Hynd, G. W. (1990). Right hemisphere dysfunction in nonverbal learning disabilities: Social, academic, and adaptive functioning in adults and children. *Psychological Bulletin, 107*, 196–209.

Share, D. L., Moffitt, T. E., & Silva, P. A. (1988). Factors associated with arithmetic and reading disabilities and specific arithmetic disability. *Journal of Learning Disabilities, 21*, 313–320.

Shipley, E. F., & Shepperson, B. (1990). Countable entities: Developmental changes. *Cognition, 34*, 109–136.

Siegel, L. S. (1974). Development of number concepts: Ordering and correspondence operations and the role of length cues. *Developmental Psychology, 10*(6), 907–912.

Siegler, R. S. (1987). The perils of averaging data over strategies: An example from children's addition. *Journal of Experimental Psychology: General, 116*, 250–264.

Simon, T. J. (1997). Reconceptualizing the origins of number knowledge: A "non-numerical" account. *Cognitive Development, 12*, 349–372.

Simon, T., Hespos, S. J., & Rochat, P. (1995). Do infants understand simple arithmetic? A replication of Wynn. *Cognitive Development, 10*, 253–269.

Simon, T. J., & Vaishnavi, S. (1996). Subitizing and counting depend on different attentional mechanisms: Evidence from visual enumeration of after-images. *Perception and Psychophysics, 58*, 915–926.

Singer, J., & Lovett, S. B. (1991, April). *Children's understanding of probability: Quantitative or directly apprehended?* Poster presented at the annual meeting of the American Education Research Association, San Francisco, California.

Smith, C., Carey, S., & Wiser, M. (1985). One differentiation: A case study of the development of the concepts of size, weight, and density. *Cognition, 21*, 177–237.

Smith, L. B. (1989). From global similarities to kinds of similarities: The construction of dimensions in development. In S. Voisniadou & A. Ortony (Eds.), *Similarity and analogical reasoning* (pp. 146–178). Cambridge, MA: Cambridge University Press.

Smith, L. B. (1993). The concept of same. In H. W. Reese (Ed.), *Advances in child development and behavior* (vol. 24, pp. 216–253). New York: Academic Press.

Smith, L. B., & Sera, M. (1992). A developmental analysis of the polar structure of dimensions. *Cognitive Psychology, 24*, 99–142.

Soja, N. N., Carey, S., & Spelke, E. S. (1991). Ontological categories guide young children's inductions of word meaning: Object terms and substance terms. *Cognition, 38*, 179–211.

Sophian, C. (1997). Beyond competence: The significance of performance for conceptual development. *Cognitive Development, 12*, 218–303.

Sophian, C., & Adams, N. (1987). Infants' understanding of numerical transformations. *British Journal of Developmental Psychology, 5*, 257–264.

Sophian, C., & Crosby, M. E. (1999, April). *Young children match spatial proportions*. Poster presented at the biennial meeting of the Society for Research in Child Development, Albuquerque, New Mexico.

Sophian, C., Garyantes, D., & Chang, C. (1997). When three is less than two: Early developments in children's understanding of fractional quantities. *Developmental Psychology, 33*, 731–744.

Sophian, C., & Wood, A. (1997). Proportional reasoning in young children: The parts and the whole of it. *Journal of Educational Psychology, 89*(2), 309–317.

Spiers, P. A. (1987). Alcalculia revisited: Current issues. In G. Deloche & X. Seron (Eds.) *Mathematical disabilities: A cognitive neuropsychological perspective* (pp. 1–25). Hillsdale, NJ: Erlbaum.

Spinillo, A. G., & Bryant, P. (1991). Children's proportional judgments: The importance of "half." *Child Development, 62*, 427–440.

Starkey, P. (1992). The early development of numerical reasoning. *Cognition, 43*, 93–126.

Starkey, P., & Cooper, R. G. Jr. (1980). Perception of numbers by human infants. *Science, 210*, 1033–1035.

Starkey, P., Spelke, E. S., & Gelman, R. (1990). Numerical abstraction by human infants. *Cognition, 36*, 97–127.

Strauss, M. S., & Curtis, L. E. (1981). Infant perception of numerosity. *Child Development, 52*, 1146–1152.

Strauss, M. S., & Curtis, L. E. (1984). Development of numerical concepts in infancy. In C. Sophian (Ed.), *Origins of cognitive skills* (pp. 131–155). Hillsdale, NJ: Erlbaum.

Taves, E. H. (1941). Two mechanisms for the perception of visual numerousness. *Archives of Psychology, 37*, 1–47.

Thelen, E., & Smith, L. B. (1994). *A dynamic systems approach to the development of cognition and action*. Cambridge, MA: MIT Press.

Tranel, D., Hall, L. E., Olson, S., & Tranel, N. N. (1987). Evidence for right-hemisphere developmental learning disability. *Developmental Neuropsychology, 3*, 113–127.

Trick, L. (1987, June). *Subitizing and canonical pattern matching*. Paper presented at the annual meeting of the Canadian Psychological Association, Vancouver, Canada.

Trick, L., & Pylyshyn, Z. (1994). Why are small and large numbers enumerated differently? A limited-capacity preattentive stage in vision. *Psychological Review, 101*, 80–102.

Uller, C., Carey, S., Huntley-Fenner, G., & Klatt, L. (1999). What representations might underlie infant numerical knowledge? *Cognitive Development,* *14,* 1–36.

Van de Walle, J. A. (1994). *Elementary school mathematics: Teaching developmentally.* 2nd ed. New York: Longman.

vanLoosbroek, E., & Smitsman, A. W. (1990). Visual perception of numerosity in infancy. *Developmental Psychology, 26,* 916–922.

Wagner, S. H., & Walters, J. (1982). A longitudinal analysis of early number concepts. In G. Foreman (Ed.) *Action and thought: From sensorimotor schemes to symbolic operations* (pp. 137–161). New York: Academic.

Wallach, L., Wall, A. J., & Anderson, L. (1967). Number conservation: The role of reversibility, addition-subtraction and misleading perceptual cues. *Child Development, 38,* 425–442.

Waxman, S. R., & Hall, D. G. (1993). The development of a linkage between count nouns and object categories: Evidence from fifteen- to twenty-one-month-old infants. *Child Development, 64,* 1224–1241.

Waxman, S. R., & Markow, D. B. (1995). Words as invitations to form categories: Evidence from 12- to 13-month-old infants. *Cognitive Psychology, 29,* 257–302.

Waxman, S. R., & Senghas, A. (1992). Relations among word meanings in early lexical development. *Developmental Psychology, 28,* 862–873.

Wynn, K. (1990). Children's understanding of counting. *Cognition, 36,* 155–193.

Wynn, K. (1992, August 27). Addition and subtraction by human infants. *Nature, 358,* 749–750.

Wynn, K. (1993, March). *Infants' ability to compute numerical transformations.* Paper presented at the biennial meeting of the Society for Research in Child Development, New Orleans, Louisiana.

Wynn, K. (1995). Origins of numerical knowledge. *Mathematical Cognition, 1*(1), 35–60.

Wynn, K. (1996). Infants' individuation and enumeration of actions. *Psychological Science, 7*(3), 164–169.

Wynn, K. (1997). Competence models of numerical development. *Cognitive Development, 12,* 333–339.

Wynn, K. (1998). Psychological foundations of number: Numerical competence in human infants. *Trends in Cognitive Science, 2*(8), 296–303.

Xu, F., & Carey, S. (1996). Infants' metaphysics: The case of numerical identity. *Cognitive Psychology, 30,* 111–153.

Index